The Myth of the Age of Entitlement

JAMES CAIRNS

THE
THE AGE
ENTITLE

MYTH OF
OF
MENT

MILLENNIALS, AUSTERITY, AND HOPE

UNIVERSITY OF TORONTO PRESS

utppublishing.com

Library and Archives Canada Cataloguing in Publication

Cairns, James Irvine, 1979–, author
  The myth of the age of entitlement: millennials, austerity, and hope
/ James Cairns.

Includes bibliographical references and index.
Issued in print and electronic formats.
ISBN 978-1-4426-3638-5 (hardcover).—ISBN 978-1-4426-3637-8 (softcover).—
ISBN 978-1-4426-3639-2 (PDF).—ISBN 978-1-4426-3640-8 (HTML)

  1. Generation Y—Political activity. 2. Young adults—Political activity.
3. Conflict of generations. 4. Entitlement attitudes. 5. Identity politics.
6. Political participation. 7. Generation Y—Social conditions. 8. Young adults—Social conditions—21st century. I. Title.

HQ799.9.P6C35 2017   305.242   C2017–900691–6
                                             C2017–900692–4

We welcome comments and suggestions regarding any aspect of our publications—please feel free to contact us at news@utphighereducation.com or visit our Internet site at www.utppublishing.com.

North America
5201 Dufferin Street
North York, Ontario, Canada, M3H 5T8

2250 Military Road
Tonawanda, New York, USA, 14150

ORDERS PHONE: 1-800-565-9523
ORDERS FAX: 1-800-221-9985
ORDERS E-MAIL: utpbooks@utpress.utoronto.ca

UK, Ireland, and continental Europe
NBN International
Estover Road, Plymouth, PL6 7PY, UK
ORDERS PHONE: 44 (0) 1752 202301
ORDERS FAX: 44 (0) 1752 202333
ORDERS E-MAIL:
enquiries@nbninternational.com

This book is printed on paper containing 100% post-consumer fibre.

The University of Toronto Press acknowledges the financial support for its publishing activities of the Government of Canada through the Canada Book Fund.

Printed in the United States of America.

CONTENTS

ACKNOWLEDGEMENTS

This book was born out of conversations with superstar filmmaker, activist, and public intellectual Brett Story. Brett's ways of thinking, her art, her way with words, and the vastness of her care, have been endless sources of inspiration and strength. I will be forever thankful that the book was finished in conversations with her, too.

I'm deeply grateful to everyone who shared their time and ideas with me during my research. Thanks especially to the dozens of millennials I interviewed in Brantford, Toronto, Ottawa, Montreal, New York, and Louisiana. My critique of the myth of the age of entitlement and my understanding of the power of millennial movements for social and environmental justice came to life through insights selflessly shared by Laurier Brantford students, Black Lives Matter activists, baristas, Bernie Sanders supporters, SHOREliners, Assembly of Se7en Generations leaders, and many, many more. Laurier student Mary-Katherine Boss was an excellent research assistant.

Huge and arm-flappingly affectionate thanks to Anne Brackenbury, my editor at the University of Toronto Press. I am extremely fortunate to have collaborated with Anne, who brings clarity, nuance, and punch to her projects even while pushing ideas into new intellectual terrain. Anne helped shape this project from the start; her rich political and literary insights are everywhere in this book. To Anna Del Col, Beate Schwirtlich, Julia Cadney, and everyone else at UTP who made this book happen: thank you, thank you, thank you! I'm grateful to Leanne Rancourt for strengthening my words through copyediting, and for Nick Craine's cover illustration.

I owe an unpayable debt of gratitude to my friends, colleagues, and comrades who provided feedback on earlier drafts of the manuscript. Among those who read major sections of the book or offered wise comments are Kate Cairns, Rick Cairns, David Calnitksy, Sue Ferguson, David McNally, Mike Rigglesford, Julie Satow, Alan Sears, Dan Snaith, Brett Story, and Cordelia Strube. Thank you also to UTP's anonymous reviewers for providing direction at different stages of the project.

I'm happy to share my gratitude for people at three places where this book was written. Thank you to Melanie Locay for supporting my 2015–2016 Allen Room residency at the New York Public Library. Thanks to Lisa Cristinzo and the staff at Artscape Gibraltar Point for making me feel at home there in August 2015. Thanks also to my many friends and interlocutors who are also my colleagues at Laurier Brantford, thank you for nourishing our workplace with big ideas, struggles for equity and democracy, and an unusual amount of fun.

Finally, all my love to the Cairns Bears, some of whom are Meadow Mice, and some of whom have names like Allen, Chivers, Dougan, Parliament, and Story. All the good bits in this book, and for that matter anything I've ever managed to think or do, are because of you. The bad bits aren't your fault.

CHAPTER ONE

THE AGE OF ENTITLEMENT?

THE MYTH

In early November 2015, 27-year-old Joel Pavelski asked his boss for a week off work. He said he needed to attend a friend's funeral in Wisconsin. Pavelski was director of programming at Mic, a New York–based news organization "created by and for millennials" (Widdicombe 2016). He got the time off, and he did go to Wisconsin— but he made up the part about the funeral. What he actually did with his week off was go to the forest and hang out with his brother. Then he blogged about it.

"I said that I was leaving town for a funeral, but I lied," wrote Pavelski (2015) in a blogpost titled "How to lose your mind and build a treehouse." He wrote about experiencing "burnout" at work and the therapeutic qualities of spending time in "the ruins of a fort that I built in the woods long ago." Pavelski's coworkers saw the blog while he was away. So did his boss.

Four months later, a journalist at the *New York Times* used Pavelski's story to introduce an article called "What Happens When Millennials Run the Workplace?" (Widdicombe 2016). It asked how bosses cope with a new generation of workers suffering from "a sense of **entitlement**, a tendency to overshare on social media, and frankness bordering on insubordination." The reporter acknowledged that

Pavelski was not the first worker to lie to his employer. "But inventing a friend's funeral, when in fact he was building a treehouse—then blogging and tweeting about it to be sure everyone at the office noticed? That feels new." The article portrayed the Pavelski affair as yet more evidence that millennials have ushered in an historic "age of entitlement."

Over the past decade, a powerful myth about the millennial generation has taken shape and spread. The myth goes something like this: Young people today, more than at any point in history, take for granted the bounty they've inherited and expect to have praise and a good life handed to them without having to do anything in return. I'm guessing you've heard the myth before; perhaps you've repeated it yourself. It often involves the morally corrosive effects of new technologies, helicopter parenting, reality TV, and other consumer trends. Like any good myth, this one is malleable, able to fit the needs of the story-teller. And what a lot of storytellers there are: politicians, professors, and reporters; bosses and TV producers; coworkers in break rooms, family at holiday dinners. The **myth of the age of entitlement** is sounded from many mouthpieces.

There are three core assumptions supporting the age of entitlement myth. First, millennials are assumed to be uniquely entitled, historically entitled—entitled like we've never seen before. Cultural critic Kristin Dombek (2016, 10) recently identified a growing fear that we're living through an unprecedented "epidemic of narcissism." Acknowledging self-centeredness in past generations does not stop scholars and bloggers alike from asserting that "ours is a moment in history that is, more than any other, absolutely exceptional" (11). In the myth of the age of entitlement, the excessive expectations of millennials exceed those even of their self-important baby boomer parents. Millennial entitlement is a whole new species of self-obsession.

Second, the myth assumes that young people have never had it so good. Smartphones, gap-years, TV on demand. Organic fast food at the click of an app. Flex hours and Facebook, hot tubs on campus, not to mention puppy-therapy rooms. Has there ever been a group of young people so pampered? Businesses spend millions of dollars trying to give fickle millennial consumers what they want (Court 2016). Millennials have been coddled by Everyone-Gets-a-Trophy parenting at home and youth-friendly management strategies in the workplace. Yet still millennials whine. Nothing is ever good enough for Generation Me.

The third assumption of the age of entitlement myth is that the epidemic of millennial narcissism isn't only annoying but a serious threat to the proper functioning of society. Millennial workers are said to threaten economic productivity. They resist authority on the job while expecting high pay, lots of time off, and unprecedented decision-making power. Coddled college students are accused of degrading institutions of higher education by demanding trigger warnings to avoid issues they don't feel like dealing with. Millennials say they care about the environment, but they go on driving cars and replacing iPhones by the bazillion. They say they want to change the world, but they're less likely than their parents to join a political party. The myth assumes that young people's excessive expectations threaten the financial and moral health of Western democracy.

This book debunks the myth of the age of entitlement. I show that this common sense story about Generation Y is both inaccurate and serves anti-democratic interests. I refer to the story as a "myth" because a myth is more complicated than a straightforward lie. The *Oxford English Dictionary* (OED 2016c) defines a myth as "a widespread but untrue or erroneous story or belief; a widely held misconception; a misrepresentation of the truth." In other words, a myth is a way of making sense of the world that provides explanations that feel true in important ways, and that may even trade in bundles of truth, despite ultimately distorting what's actually going on.

It's easy to find Joel Pavelski–style examples of young people acting selfishly, taking advantage of others, claiming special privileges. It's true that millennials spend a lot of time on social media creating online identities that express conceptions of themselves. It's a fact that millennials are living longer with their parents than did young people in previous generations. To reject the myth of the age of entitlement doesn't require denying these truths. It requires challenging the tendency of these truths to be packaged into a neat and tidy story about how millennials are coddled, self-absorbed, addicted to social media, and hopelessly dependent on mommy and daddy. When a fuller range of millennial experiences are analyzed in relation to broader economic, political, and cultural trends, it becomes clear that there isn't a generalized problem of inflated expectations. The prevailing description and explanation of millennial experiences is a myth: a widely held misconception.

If it were only that the myth got the facts wrong, the misconception would not be so troubling. Correct a few errors here and there, and now the ledger is balanced. The problem is that the myth not only makes factual errors, but it delegitimizes the notion that young people are right to expect better than the status quo. The myth of the age of entitlement both describes expressions of entitlement on the rise and judges that the trend is harmful. It supports a vision of society in which people have a responsibility to lower their expectations. In light of the historic hardships faced by millennials, which include the decline of well-paid, secure jobs with benefits and a pension; cuts to social services; skyrocketing student debt; and an unprecedented ecological crisis, it is deeply problematic to suggest that the biggest problem with young people today is that they expect too much.

In contrast to the idea that society is plagued by the excessive expectations of young people, millennial activist and writer Sarah Leonard (2016, 3) argues that "we need a vision of a better future, one that turns our modern capacity for abundant food, shelter, and health into a guarantee that no one will suffer for their lack." People are entitled to have their needs met, writes Leonard, regardless of what's in their bank account. The myth of the age of entitlement says young people have been given too much already. They are entitled to nothing more than what they can afford to buy. They should be more grateful for what they have. No, Leonard says: Millennials and the generations who follow them are entitled to much better than they're getting.

Do not misinterpret my argument by assuming that I intend to replace a myth of millennial entitlement with a myth of millennial heroism. Our world and our lives are complex and full of contradictions. The best social research recognizes both the tidy patterns and the tangled messes that arise from billions of people sharing lives and the natural environment. Half a century ago the critical theorist Herbert Marcuse (1964) described how the interlocking economic, political, and technological imperatives of mass modern society close down spaces for experiencing and cultivating our full human potential. Millennials have come of age during a period in which the material and emotional burdens of survival have been even more aggressively downloaded onto the individual (Berlant 2011; Raynor 2016; Sears 2014). Of course these individualizing forces inform contemporary youth cultures, but they don't mechanically produce a generation of narcissists. There's no need for a cartoon version of the Millennial Savior to argue that hope for a new era of social and ecological justice lies in youth-led movements encouraging masses of people to raise their expectations, feel entitled to having needs met, and refuse to settle for less.

GENERATION ME, ME, ME!

In the *Times* of London, historian Amanda Foreman (2014) asks, "Mirror, mirror on the wall, who is the most narcissistic, entitled and lazy of them all?" Her response: "there's no contest: it's the Millennial Generation—those 18 to 35-year olds who text instead of talk, who have a shorter concentration span than my dog Max, who believe that rules are just guidelines and who know beyond all doubt that they are unique and special human beings."

Corporate leaders describe millennials as "impatient and self-absorbed," their "unreasonable sense of entitlement" making them deaf to traditional working principles, such as "paying your dues" (Gupta-Sunderji 2014). Millennials want to be rich but don't want to work; they're "too medicated for their own good"; they move back home after school to enjoy "amenities that rarely come with a cheap starter apartment"; they look for workplaces "that feel a little like Fraternity Row" (Wieczner 2014). Academic entitlement—"the expectation that one should receive certain positive academic outcomes ... independent of performance"—is said to be a mounting problem on campus (Kopp et al. 2011, 107). Millennial students expect their professors "to go to exceptional lengths" to meet their demands (Greenberger et al. 2008, 1193), exhibiting worrisome entitled behavior likely to "extend to the employee environment" (Boesveld 2014).

The twentysomethings on HBO's hit TV show *Girls* lack initiative and respect for authority, yet they moan about how hard it is to get ahead. Their expectations of spacious apartments and expensive dinners are unmatched by the work ethic necessary to land a job that could pay for those things. As *Salon* journalist Anna North (2013) writes, "the show confirms what many already think about millennials: that they're demanding brats, emotionally hobbled by hook-up culture and financially supported by their parents."

Lena Dunham's creations are hardly unique pop culture depictions of Generation Y. On *Broad City*, Abbi and Ilana's biggest problems are scoring weed and figuring out how to talk to hot guys. The Kardashians, real millennials (or *reality* millennials, at least), whine about the imperfections of their lucrative public appearances and celebrity boyfriends. The film *Fort Tilden*, a 2015 "send up of millennial culture," stars the twentysomething Harper, "a nightmare of a person, a sociopath with whom you'd never want to spend time," trying to get to the beach (Walsh 2015). Ryan from *The Office* and Cerie from *30 Rock* are so absorbed with their social lives and cell phones they can barely communicate with their office supervisors. Real-life human resources expert Susan Heathfield (2015) advises that "Gen Y was raised by doting parents in a world that centered around them and their needs.[...] They want praise, praise, praise and thank you."

Blame MTV for surging millennial entitlement, says *Wall Street Journal* columnist Jeffrey Zaslow. Blame "the state of California, Burger King, Fed-Ex ... and parents, especially parents" (Zaslow 2007b). Zaslow (2007a) once wrote an article called "Blame It on Mr. Rogers: Why Young Adults Feel so Entitled." The children's TV show host, writes Zaslow, is guilty of inflating millennials' egos because he "told several generations of children that they were 'special' just for being whoever they were."

The leading scholar of contemporary entitlement culture is Jean M. Twenge. A professor at San Diego State University and, in the words of the *New York Times*, a "celebrity psychologist" (Quenqua 2013), Twenge has written two books about the crisis of entitlement in the United States: *The Narcissism Epidemic: Living in the Age of Entitlement* (2009, with W. Keith Campbell), and *Generation Me: Why Today's Young Americans Are More Confident, Assertive, Entitled—And More Miserable than Ever Before* (2014). Her many academic articles on the subject have titles like "The Evidence for Generation Me and Against Generation We" and "Generational Changes and Their Impact in the Classroom: Teaching Generation Me." Twenge's work synthesizes and elaborates on much of the underdeveloped griping about millennial entitlement found in news articles and political debate.

Twenge uses survey research and cultural analysis to conclude that "the Millennials are the most narcissistic generation in history" (2014, 70). Twenge and Campbell (2009, 18) define a narcissist as someone with "an overinflated view of his own abilities [...]. Narcissists see themselves as fundamentally superior—they are special, entitled, and unique." Prior to the 1970s, they argue, people were less entitled and more community minded. This showed itself in large ways, like the emphasis on "freedom and equality" as core American values, as opposed to the contemporary emphasis on self-expression (57). It manifested in small ways, too, like giving babies traditional names, rather than the ostentatiously unique ones given to many babies in the twenty-first century (see Chapter 11 of Twenge and Campbell 2009).

The exact year in which millennials started and stopped being born differs depending on who you ask. The Pew Research Center (2016) defines the millennial generation as "those born after 1980 and the first generation to come of age in the new millennium." The sociologists Neil Howe and William Strauss (2000) say the millennial era began in 1982. Others say it started in 1977 and ended in 1995 (Lyall 2016). For reasons that will become clear, I'm skeptical about generational analysis. Let's say the millennial era started around 1980. The important question is, Why do millennial-bashers say that Gen Y developed and spread the entitlement epidemic?

First, Twenge and Campbell (2009) blame a new style of parenting. Parents are too permissive, give children too much authority, protect them from teachers' criticisms, and shower them with unearned praise. Parents have given children all sorts of new freedoms, powers, and consumer goods, without requiring that children take on the concomitant responsibilities. Career advisors now report millennials expecting "lots of cool perks and benefits to make their job feel more rewarding" (O'Donnell 2015).

Second, contemporary celebrity culture treats narcissism as a virtue. Celebs prattle on about self-improvement, being true to oneself,

self-motivation, self-branding. They name clothing lines and colognes after themselves. The very public lives of celebrities like Miley Cyrus, Kanye West, and the Kardashians are models of self-absorption and greed. People see the wealth and fame of the ruthless Donald Trump, then mimic the way he treats people on *The Apprentice* (to say nothing of his performance as president).

Third, new technologies intensify negative trends. Social media and rising entitlement have formed "a feedback loop, with narcissistic people seeking out ways to promote themselves on the Web and those same websites encouraging narcissism even among the more humble" (Twenge and Campbell 2009, 107). Psychiatrist Keith Ablow (2013) argues that millennials' addiction to Facebook, Twitter, and other social media turns them into "faux celebrities—the equivalent of lead actors in their own fictionalized life stories." The *Huffington Post* reported that "Millennials Are Surprisingly Chill with Funeral Selfies" (Moye 2015). It shares concerns about the "Me, Me, Me Generation," as Gen Y was dubbed by Joel Stein (2013) in a *Time* magazine cover story. In Stein's words, "technology has only exacerbated" the problem of millennial "selfishness."

The past 10 years have seen a steady rise in fear of Gen Y's rising expectations. Dozens of books have been published with titles like *The Entitlement Trap* (Eyre and Eyre 2011), *The Trophy Kids Grow Up* (Alsop 2008), *The Life of I* (Manne 2014), and *Not Everyone Gets a Trophy: How to Manage the Millennials* (Tulgan 2009). They echo Twenge and Campbell's age of entitlement narrative, promising to help parents, employers, and teachers figure out what to do with a generation of young people that demands so much more than what's reasonable.

GENERATION SCREWED

Paradoxically, at the same time critics have been banging alarm bells about millennial entitlement gone wild, millions of millennials have actually been *dis*entitled on numerous fronts (Barr and Malik 2016). Youth unemployment is near record highs in many places, and everywhere the jobs available to Gen Y are increasingly part-time contract work without benefits, pensions, or employment security (Burrell and

Setzer 2015; Grant 2014). Since 1990, the cost of living has gone up 67 per cent while the real value of the minimum wage has increased by only 21 per cent (Gilson 2011). Real (inflation-adjusted) wages continue to decline, meaning that even as the dollar amount paid to workers may increase slightly, their purchasing power has fallen (Blades 2015). Between 2007 and 2013, American workers between the ages of 18 and 34 saw their take-home pay fall (Levitz 2016). No wonder *Time* reports that "millennials are setting new records for living with their parents" (Alter 2015). Canada's minister of finance recently said that "short-term contract work will continue and young adults should get used to it" (Carrick 2016).

Decades of government cutbacks to social services have sent the price students pay for postsecondary education skyrocketing—and with it student debt. Even after being adjusted for inflation, average debt by borrower in the United States doubled between 1993 and 2014, from $15,000 to $33,000 (Izzo 2014). The economic prospects for millennials who don't attend college are even bleaker. A study by the Pew Research Center (Drake 2014) showed that "millennials are the first in the modern era to have higher levels of student loan debt, poverty and unemployment, and lower levels of wealth and personal income than their two immediate predecessor generations had at the same age."

And the Earth has become less livable during the millennial era. Between 1980 and 2015 the average global surface temperature rose from 0.28 degrees Celsius to 0.87 degrees Celsius (NASA 2015). Climate scientists warn of the potential of total ecological collapse should average temperatures reach 2 degrees Celsius. Without rapid, major changes to how corporations are entitled to run their operations, 2 degrees could be reached during millennial lifetimes. Even some business-friendly reporters have had to admit that "young people really do have it harder today" (Carrick 2012).

On the indie-media site AlterNet, Alex Henderson (2013) includes "the post-9/11 surveillance state" as one of "10 reasons millennials are the screwed generation." In his words, "Between the use of torture on political detainees at Guantanamo, the Patriot Act, warrantless wiretapping, the National Defense Authorization Act, false politics on the Terrorist Screening Center's No-Fly List, and intrusive TSA searches at airports, Millennials have spent their adult lives in an era in which constitutional liberties are under constant attack in the name of fighting terrorism." Because of the racist assumptions built into the surveillance state, millennials of color face especially severe threats to their liberty. The incarceration rate has soared in the millennial era, disproportionately dispossessing black, Latino, and Indigenous millennials of present and future freedom (Davis 2003).

Millennial students, artists, activists, and workers have led the charge to show that real socioeconomic trends mean that, far from being coddled members of Generation Me, many young people are hardly scraping by as members of what would be better named "Generation Less" (Raynor 2016; see also Caruso 2014; Crockett and StudentNation 2013). In a *Salon* series by feminists of color, cultural critic and performer Sydette Harry (2013) condemns the myth of the age of entitlement for lumping all millennials into the same category— one that appears to assume that all young people are white, middle-class city dwellers. In reality, Harry notes, millennials "are a diverse group, who have had extraordinarily different experiences growing up." If we want to understand "the real story of millennials," she writes, we need to examine "the startling inequalities both between and within genera- tions." There have obviously been tremendous changes in how people communicate, work, and play over the past 30 years. It makes sense to ask *what's new* about Generation Y. But by treating era-of-birth as the core determinant of ideas and behavior, the myth of the age of entitlement ignores inequalities running along lines of race, class, and gender that are far more powerful in shaping people's experiences and life chances than is shared generational membership.

Sociologist Susan McDaniel (2001) introduces the concept of "gendered generations" to deepen our thinking about how age cohorts are internally diverse. Feminist scholars and activists use the term *pa- triarchy* to describe a social system like that of the modern West, in which "men hold predominant authority in business and the state, with a near-monopoly of top positions. Men and boys tend to control public spaces such as streets and playgrounds. Men hold authority in many families and institutions of civil society," and men (with the exception of queer and trans men) are "relatively free from rape and serious domestic violence" (Connell 2014, 246). Sexism, racism, and economic inequality continue to mean that some millennials are far more effectively entitled to having their needs met than others.

Andrew Boryga (2016), a millennial, draws on his own experience in an article about how the age of entitlement storyline ignores the routine hardships faced by many immigrants and people of color:

> My story hardly reflects an "entitled" and "narcissistic" upbringing. Mom came here at age 17 from Puerto Rico, saving all her pennies after working 30 hours a week on an assembly line during high school. When she arrived, with little grasp of English and American culture, she was robbed of all her cash before she made it out of the airport. By age 30, she was divorced with three kids. We had hoopties and some bare Christmases. From age five until 22, I shared a bedroom with my twin sisters in the Bronx.

Trustworthy arguments about rising or falling millennial expectations and standards of living must attend to the structural **disentitlement** of women, people of color, poor people, and other systematically disadvantaged groups.

"MORE AND MORE CRAPPIER AND MORE AND MORE EXPENSIVE"

I first became curious about the age of entitlement myth while conducting interviews with millennial students on my campus in 2012–13.[1] It was a socially turbulent time. The economy was still reeling from the Great Recession of 2008–09. Mass movements for greater democracy and

---

1 Laurier Brantford is a campus of Wilfrid Laurier University, an hour west of Toronto, Ontario. At its founding in 1999, the campus was home to 38 students and 2 faculty in one interdisciplinary bachelor of arts program. Today it is home to over 3,000 students and 60 full-time faculty spanning more than 15 programs (including three master of arts degrees). When my focus groups were conducted, close to a third of Laurier Brantford students were completing a joint BA/BEd program (doing the education part of their degree at the Brantford campus of Nipissing University). Fittingly, 8 of the 25 interview participants were enrolled in the concurrent education program.

equality were gaining strength and attracting public attention. Dictators were being overthrown by mass insurgencies in the Arab world. Labor unions and community organizations shut down the Wisconsin legislature in a popular struggle for worker rights. The Occupy movement for genuine democracy had spread from Manhattan to more than 180 cities around the world. Hundreds of thousands of people in Quebec were marching in the streets in support of a months-long student strike against a plan to hike college tuition by 75 per cent.

In this period of social upheaval, I wanted to better understand what young people felt about their situation as students and workers, and how they imagined life after graduation. So I tacked up posters on campus offering free pizza to student volunteers willing to talk about their experiences and ideas. By the end of the spring term in 2013 I'd interviewed 25 students in groups of five (for my full results, see Cairns 2015).[2]

Students began the focus groups individually filling out a short questionnaire. One question asked for three words to describe the current job market. In the group discussion that followed, descriptions were overwhelmingly negative, albeit linguistically creative: bleak, dire, nonexistent, competitive, scary, low paying, no security, impossible, "utter shit." Heather, reflecting on beginning to look for full-time work after graduation, talked about the demoralizing task of applying for demanding but low-paying work:

> And then, it's just, like, very intimidating to read those descriptions for jobs, and then you go down and look at the salary and it's like $18,000 [*knowing "hmms" from other participants*]—minus your housing—and you're like, Oh! OK! Give me a second to think about that. Because I have about *how much* in student fees next year? I'm paying off my OSAP [student loan] and it's a good, like, ten grand or something next year ... so, you know, that's half my funds. So I don't know. It's just scary, right?

---

2 All students were between 18 and 25 and self-identified as growing up in "working-class" or "middle-class" households. Some claimed to follow politics more closely than others, but none belonged to a political party or identified as an activist.

As an immigrant to Canada, Sofia watched her parents struggle for years to achieve a decent living standard with some security, "but it was really, really, really hard for them. And now for them to tell me that I'm going to have it even harder … it scares me so much." In the words of one student, the bleak job market is in addition to the fact that "in healthcare and education it seems like things are getting more and more crappier and more and more expensive." She said that vision care and Pap smears used to be covered by public health care, but now patients had to pay out of pocket for these and other services.

The experiences of students made it easy to understand why frustration and fear were common themes in our discussions. They were swimming in debt. They'd struggled to find work while watching family members get laid off. I expected students to demand big changes to help them navigate the harsh socioeconomic climate. But they appeared not to feel as though they deserved anything different. These were not the whiny, demanding teens I'd seen on TV shows like *Gossip Girl*. They didn't sound anything like the ideal narcissistic millennial described in Twenge's books. The students I talked with felt entitled to very little when it came to meeting their material and emotional needs.

When asked what could be done to improve the situation, students talked about needing to lower their expectations about wages and benefits; being willing to work outside their area of interest; needing to move to different parts of the province, the country, the world. They emphasized the importance of networking. "No one's going to hand you a job," was said often, "you've got to get out there and hustle." But doesn't this seem unfair, I asked? Don't people deserve to do the work they're passionate about in the place they love to live? Everyone in Michael's group nodded when he waved away my suggestion: "I don't know … it's just … this is reality."

None of them liked the bleak job market they presumed they would be facing or the rising cost of school, food, and rent or cuts to health and social services. But they expressed no sense of entitlement to even basic social supports, to say nothing of suggesting that they deserved more expansive social rights. Sociologist Jennifer Silva (2013, 10) writes that for working-class people today, adulthood is increasingly defined by "low expectations of work, wariness toward romantic commitment, widespread distrust of social institutions,

[and] profound isolation from others." Facing mounting economic and social obstacles, many millennials are resigned to settle for less. Yet stories and images of hyperentitled young people continue to fill the mass media and scholarly journals. The age of entitlement myth has formed part of our collective common sense. Why has an age of disentitlement become represented as its opposite?

THE POLITICS OF DESERVINGNESS

The myth of the age of entitlement must be taken seriously because it not only describes young people but expresses a value judgment about what they deserve. It advances a normative agenda, a political–ethical claim about what it is reasonable or excessive for people to expect. To define millennials as the entitled generation isn't just to say that they have high expectations; it's to say that their expectations are *too high* and that young people *ought* to settle for less.

In 2016, Frederick was a sophomore and social justice activist at Columbia University in New York City. Between bites of a cheeseburger in the upstairs seating section of his favorite campus deli, he expressed concerns about which groups are hurt most at his school by the myth of the age of entitlement:

> There's definitely a segment of this generation that is the entitled, millennial segment. But that's in every generation. [...] The problem is that there's also so much suffering going on in our generation, because of exploitation and oppression, and it gets silenced, it gets thrown under the rug, when you just say "millennials are entitled." The university can just write off the Fight for $15 movement—which is trying to put food on low-income students' plates—by just saying, you know, "All these students have millionaire parents, and they're just whining to get more money." (Personal communication)

Neither Twenge nor her most prominent critics name the high stakes that Frederick rightly identifies: that is, the **politics of**

entitlement. By that term I mean struggles over what it is reasonable to deserve and where to draw the line between deserving and undeserving. These struggles play out on both the level of ideas and the level of physical access to resources.

Drawing lines between deserving and undeserving matters a lot in our individual lives. The boss who says no to posting the schedule a bit earlier; the prof who allows students to rewrite the exam; parents who are or aren't convinced to serve a tofu turkey at the next holiday meal: Millennials grapple with different views on deservingness every day. However, my ultimate interest in the age of entitlement myth goes far beyond the way in which overentitlement gets defined in individual cases. I'm interested in what particular struggles over the so-called problem of youth entitlement tell us about broad struggles that shape society.

The age of entitlement narrative and the counternarratives that challenge it contain and advance competing answers to the most wide-ranging social questions: How should society operate? What institutions and values are required to achieve social justice? Whose interests and needs get fully counted in our communities; whose interests and needs get discounted? The questions are as daunting as they are essential and urgent. What is really getting played out in debates about millennial entitlement is a clash between different visions of society.

The vision associated with the age of entitlement narrative promotes private property rights and consumer relations, the allocation of resources through buying and selling. In this view, the market is the key mechanism for making the best decisions for individuals and society. You are entitled to exchange your skills and labor power for the best price you can get for them. And you are entitled to use the money you earn to consume however you like. Citizens are first and foremost consumers. Freedom is the freedom to choose from options available on the market. You are entitled to what you are able to buy and sell; nothing more, nothing less.

From this perspective, a certain amount of social inequality is inevitable and desirable. Some people are smarter or stronger or work harder than others, and the strong ones will always get more. Competition drives innovation. If you were entitled to having your needs met, you'd have no incentive to compete, no reason to contribute to the community. Society would break down. Maintaining a healthy social order depends on resources being allocated through market transactions. Necessarily, there will be winners and losers, but everyone is entitled to compete.

In sharp contrast, there is a vision of society that rejects market fundamentalism and how it gets promoted through the age of entitlement myth. This alternative vision aspires to a future based in more expansive social rights and democratic decision making. Social rights are goods, services, and protections accessible to everyone, regardless of their ability to pay: for example, "the right to an adequate standard of living, including adequate food, clothing and housing," the right to form and join trade unions, and the right to education (Amnesty International 2016). In this view, everyone is entitled to having basic needs and desires met.

The social rights view sees a healthy society as the result of complex "social interdependence" (Keane 2000, 9). Rich companies and people depend on an endlessly sprawling system of workers and natural resources to make their money. Wealth is produced socially and therefore ought to be shared more evenly across society. It is fair and right, then, for strong redistributional policies to support institutions that meet the needs of all.

In this view, everyone is also entitled to participate in the decision-making processes that affect their lives locally and in relation to the broader world. The potential mechanisms of deep democracy are many: democratic workplace councils, student assemblies, representative legislatures, neighborhood committees, as well as city-wide and country-wide referenda. Questions of which ones work best are crucial and can be vexing. Nevertheless, the assumption remains: Everyone deserves—*is entitled*—to play a role in choosing and guiding policies that affect us all. The best decisions will be ones that emerge from the experiences and wisdom of the people themselves in conditions of freedom and equality.

In recent debates over so-called millennial entitlement, the choice between these contending visions of society is rarely stated so starkly or in as much detail. But the stakes in debates over the age of entitlement storyline are no less significant than the question of what sort of society we want for ourselves and for future generations.

MULTIPLE MEANINGS

Political scientist Daniel Bell addressed the **politics of entitlement** head-on in a 1975 article called the "The Revolution of Rising Entitlements." Writing at the peak of what social scientists refer to as "the broad welfare state" period (see Sears 2003, 44), Bell was angrily responding to the expansion of social rights won through mass movement struggles in the 1950s and 1960s. The welfare state attempted to satisfy some basic needs of all citizens through publicly funded income support programs and services in education, housing, health, and other fields. In the broad welfare state period, there was historic expansion in both the number of people accessing full citizenship rights and what citizenship rights entitled you to. Although this was years before the first millennials were born, Bell pulled a linguistic trick that's become routine in today's anti–Gen Y rhetoric: He blended different meanings of the word *entitlement*.

The *Oxford English Dictionary* (OED 2016a) provides several different definitions of the word. Probably the one used most commonly is the negative meaning, as in the millennial "sense of entitlement" referred to by Twenge and other critics: "the belief that one is inherently deserving of privileges or special treatment." The word can also refer to "a legal right or just claim to do, receive, or possess something." This meaning involves a sense of entitlement too, but one based on legitimate rather than spurious claims. Third, the word *entitlement* can refer to "a service, benefit, or payment granted to an eligible party through a government programme." Minimum wage, a limit to the number of hours employers can require you to work, free elementary and secondary schooling, social security, and Medicare all fall under this broad category of state and workplace entitlements.

As Linguist Geoff Nunberg (2012) observes, a powerful political weapon is forged when the negative meaning implied by "sense of entitlement" is combined with reference to entitlement programs such as welfare or social security. Schooling, transportation, health care, and all the other things people need to survive are more easily reframed as privileges that individual consumers should be responsible for securing through their personal bank accounts, rather than the basics that everyone deserves, which will be funded collectively. Bell's article is a virtuoso performance of this sleight of hand.

Bell argued that citizen claims for health care, equal pay for women, unemployment insurance, pensions, and welfare are selfish and destructive because they will lead to economic breakdown. He was attacking the new rights and protections won by mass movements of the 1960s. Bell said that pressure from "interest groups" threatened to "overload" the political system, "to confront it with far more grievances than legislators and judges know how to cope with" (Bell 1975, 103). The threat was severe: If people don't lower their expectations about the standard of living they feel entitled to, the government will be bankrupt and broken in no time, crushed under the weight of rising entitlements. The sentiment was crystalized in a speech by the US president played by Kevin Spacey on the TV show *House of Cards* (Mankiewicz 2015): "We've been crippled by Social Security, Medicare, Medicaid, by welfare, by entitlements," says Spacey's President Frank Underwood. "And that is the root of the problem: entitlements. Let me be clear: You are entitled to nothing." Spacey pauses for dramatic effect before repeating himself: "You are entitled to nothing."

Echoes of Bell are heard in the age of entitlement myth today. For example, a columnist in Canada's *Globe and Mail* says that the problem with rising postsecondary tuition isn't that the cost is prohibitively high, but that millennials think it should be lower. "The real problem isn't student debt," writes Margaret Wente (2013), "it's student expectation—the idea that a young person should be rewarded with a fulfilling, well-paying job and a middle-class lifestyle as soon as they hit the market." Career advisor J.T. O'Donnell (2015) blames millennials for expecting employers to pay for training and professional development: "Millennials should foot the bill to develop themselves and make themselves worth more to the employer." Bell accused social movement demands of being economically destructive. Millennial expectations are criticized for having the same effect.

But Bell's warning was not only about economic collapse. He said that expanding social programs and the swelling citizen expectations they reflected were also morally corrosive. He condemned social movements because of their "hedonistic emphasis on the satisfaction of private appetites, which is involved in so much of the pursuit of public goods" (182). Moralism of this sort would later drive major studies by sociologists Charles Murray (1984) and Lawrence Mead (1986), both of whom concluded that state and workplace entitlements deny people the character-building pressure to fend for themselves and the experience of succeeding by one's own ingenuity, determination, and skills.

In the tradition of Bell, Murray, and Mead, O'Donnell (2015) wrote that millennials have become "addicted to praise, perks, and other incentives" because they've had things handed to them all their lives. She says "millennials must learn to find intrinsic motivation (internal drive for work)" and stop expecting employers or anyone else to satisfy their needs. She frames being a good citizen as being a savvy, self-reliant consumer. During his 2012 run for US president, Republican Mitt Romney framed the choice facing voters as "a choice between an 'entitlement society' dependent on government welfare and an 'opportunity society' that enables business to flourish" (in Rucker 2011). In November 2016, when college students protested the election of Donald Trump, an Iowa state legislator introduced a law he called the "Suck It Up, Buttercup" Bill (Kaufmann 2016). Representative Bobby Kaufmann proclaimed he wanted an end to universities spending money "to coddle people that cannot handle the election results."

One of the most insidious things about the age of entitlement myth is that it's used to explain not only the questionable decisions of the Joel Pavelskis of the world but millennial expectations of all kinds. Gen Y's soaring sense of entitlement becomes the explanation when millennial workers hold "unrealistic expectations about career progression" (Andersen 2016). Yet the same anti-entitlement reasoning is used to dismiss supposedly overly sensitive millennial students campaigning against racist Halloween costumes on campus (Castellanos 2015). The millennial CEO of Snapchat refuses to sell his company for billions of dollars? Yet another sign of Gen Y entitlement (Mangalindan 2015).

Only when the politics of entitlement are ignored is it possible to portray each of these situations as different versions of the same phenomenon. Once we begin inquiring into the varying levels of social power held by the young people involved, and the reasons driving their entitlement claims, it becomes possible to ask whether in certain circumstances expecting better treatment than what's on offer is not only not necessarily a bad thing, but is actually essential to fighting inequality and deepening democracy.

DEMOCRACY DEPENDS ON ENTITLEMENT

Sonia Singh is an organizer with the Workers Action Centre (WAC) in Toronto. The WAC is a worker-based organization that supports and advocates on behalf of especially precarious working people. Most WAC members are nonunionized workers, and many are recent immigrants, workers of color, women, and young people. Singh played an instrumental role in the WAC-led campaign for a $14 minimum wage in Ontario. According to the campaign, the existing minimum wage of $11 per hour "leaves full-time workers more than 16% below the poverty line" (Workers Action Centre 2016). Singh told me that at her organization's meetings workers have long condemned the existing minimum wage rate for leaving them unable to maintain even a basic standard of living (personal communication). She often hears workers saying "it should be our right not to be living in poverty when we're earning minimum wage."

I suggested to Singh that this is precisely the sort of sentiment that gets interpreted by some as a symptom of an unhealthy culture of entitlement. If people are struggling with what they're earning now, they should find higher-paying work or cut their spending. Singh responded that "it certainly involves a sense of entitlement. But in this case, it's coming from a very political, positive, rights-based sense. [...] Our members are saying, 'We're not asking for this, we're not begging for it. We're *demanding* it.' Everybody deserves either benefits or wages that they can survive on."

Twenge and the age of entitlement myth condemn "acting as if you have a title—or a right—to something even when you don't" (Twenge and Campbell 2009, 231). But history is full of examples in which just such activity is an essential part of pressing for and winning greater social justice. For example, historian of black liberation in the United

States, Komozi Woodard (2011), argues that at the root of freedom struggles among slaves in the American south was, in his words, "A sense that we are entitled to something better." As I argue in Chapter 2, the Black Lives Matter campaign that erupted in Ferguson, Missouri, and spread across the United States in 2014 is part of the tradition Woodard identifies—a tradition of demanding justice where justice has been denied. A collective feeling of being entitled to safer working conditions is part of what drove the great labor movements of the twentieth century. When the feminist scholar and activist Silvia Federici (1975) wrote of "the revolutionary implications of the demand of wages for housework," (4) she was drawing attention to the potential power of a surging sense of entitlement among women doing unpaid domestic labor. The radically democratic slogan "No One Is Illegal" is implicitly a claim about the universal entitlement not to be discriminated against on the basis of citizenship status.

Sociologist Frances Fox Piven (2006) highlights the importance of rising senses of deservingness in winning the most cherished rights and privileges in the United States. The end to chattel slavery, the universal right to vote, and crucial worker protections took hold only as a result of centuries of struggles fought by populations driven by surging **senses of entitlement** developed through collective action. A short article in *Jacobin* magazine (which, it's worth noting, is run by millennials) puts the point beautifully: "The discourse of entitlement is a discourse of rights, of human agents claiming what's theirs instead of asking permission from the powerful" (Gude 2013).

There are tensions among proponents of democracy over what sort of access to resources people living under democratic governments are entitled to. But the promise of democracy, and the demand of the leading sections of democratic revolutions like those in the United States (1776), Haiti (1791), and Russia (1917), is that *everyone* is entitled to a fair standard of living and to participate in decision making: to speak, act, and organize freely within conditions of relative equality.

The argument for *rule by the people* I make in this book envisions a more expansive model of collective self-government than provided for in existing systems of official democracy. Sociologist Alan Sears and I define *official democracy* as the political system governing countries in the contemporary Global North (Cairns and Sears 2012, 7). This model centers on representative legislatures, a sprawling bureaucracy, and private property rights. Official democracy is one version of rule by the people; but democracy has not been perfected in this version, nor can a final, ideal form of democracy ever be worked out in theory. The expansion of democracy from ancient Greece to the Arab Spring has always been driven by disadvantaged groups seeking greater control over society's resources and the opportunity to participate more fully in the decisions that matter most in their lives (Laxer 2009).

Democracy is best conceived, then, as a project that needs to be developed continuously if we're going to solve the pressing problems of inequality, unfreedom, and environmental degradation. This will certainly involve deepening democracy in elections, legislatures, and other institutions of official democracy. But it also means democratizing workplaces, schools, and ways of living together in communities large and small. Cultivating what Sears and I call "democracy from below" will draw on the best of historical traditions of rule by the people, from Iroquois democracy to liberal citizenship rights. But it will aim to transcend the limits of any existing model in the interests of providing the grounds for freedom and justice for all individuals and society as a whole.

SITUATION NORMAL

Three years after Daniel Bell attacked "the revolution of rising entitlements," American political scientist Charles Derber (1978, 26) wrote that he was encouraged by the "emerging culture of entitlement among young workers." Derber's research was based on interviews conducted with unemployed youth in the late 1970s. Their stories led Derber to conclude that years of social movement victories, a robust welfare state, and low levels of unemployment provided fertile grounds for even greater radical social critique and action to develop. In his words, "the more highly entitled worker is less likely to accept blame for discontent related to work, more likely to blame society for not assuring his or her rights, and thus more likely to be receptive to radical political interpretations of discontents" (32).

Despite their deep political differences, Bell and Derber mostly agreed that both citizens' senses of entitlement and entitlement programs expanded in the 1960s. It's just that they fundamentally disagreed about whether rising entitlements were a good or a bad thing. In stark contrast to Bell's condemnation of "the revolution of rising entitlements," which was driven by fear of the threat they posed to established political and economic institutions, Derber favored "the rise of universalistic entitlement ideology" because he favored the radicalization of youth and the possibility of genuine social transformation (34).

Over the past 40 years there hasn't been the surge in radicalization Derber hoped for. Bell's anti-entitlement perspective has been the dominant one. It is the ideological soil that has nourished the myth of the age of entitlement. However, the dominance of Bell's perspective is not necessarily evidence that where he draws the line between normal and excessive forms of deservingness is more "correct" in an abstract sense, more philosophically "right." Dominant ideas about what are normal levels of entitlement versus excessive ones aren't determined by logic or through philosophical debate. They get decided through social struggles over how people satisfy their emotional and material needs.

A colleague of mine demonstrates this point in a powerful personal story. She was born in the early 1960s to a middle-class family in which her father, a doctor, was the primary earner. When my colleague was born, her father was so certain that postsecondary education would be free by the time his newborn daughter graduated high school that he didn't bother beginning to save for her university tuition. This was not because he was foolish or bad with money; on the contrary, he was a careful family planner. His high expectations were driven by his decades-long experience of rising standards of living through expanding social rights. It was normal for him to expect the satisfaction of more and more needs through public programs.

Struggles during the decades before my colleague's birth produced an extensive system of new **legal entitlements** in the form of the welfare state. In Canada, the family allowance was established in 1944, universal pensions became available in 1951–52, and the first permanent unemployment insurance program was created in 1956. The

Canada Pension Plan, Canada Assistance Plan, and Medicare were created in the 1960s. Governments of all stripes across the Global North pursued similar policy agendas. All of these were at least in part government responses to the growing power and demands of democratic movements for workers' rights and access to full citizenship for all members of society. They also reflected state and business policymakers' fear of falling back into the sort of hardship and social conflict experienced during the Great Depression (Wolff 2012).

In this context of postwar economic boom and growing popular power, it's hardly surprising that my friend's father felt his daughter would soon be entitled to a publicly funded postsecondary education. The expansion of the welfare state meant that people *were* entitled to more than they ever had been before. Decades of struggle created a context in which it was normal, not selfish, to expect robust social rights.

The struggles that determine what is widely understood as normal or excessive levels of deservingness involve the complex interplay between senses of entitlement and legal entitlements. I use the term *senses of entitlement* to refer to feelings of deservingness. Chapter 2 explains that senses of entitlement can serve either democratic or oppressive interests. I use the term *legal entitlements* to refer to protections and guarantees recognized by law or firmly established custom. The right to vote, to profit from private property, minimum wage protections, and anti-discrimination laws are examples of current legal entitlements. Legal entitlements differ from place to place, and they change over time as laws and traditions change. If there were a way to itemize all the legal entitlements in a particular time and place, you'd end up with a picture of what I call the **real entitlement framework**. It doesn't matter that it's impossible to create such a comprehensive list. It's useful to have a term for referring to the general shape of what people are actually entitled to (and not entitled to), as opposed to what we're told we're entitled to by politicians who want to appear generous.

MILLENNIAL STRUGGLES

There's a cynical logic to the fact that millennials are being accused of having an inflated sense of entitlement at precisely the moment when social rights are disappearing. To be sure, legal entitlements bolstering democracy and social justice have been won during the last three decades. For example, the right to same-sex marriage was won in Canada and the United States after decades of struggle by LGBTQ people for full citizenship. Indigenous peoples' rights to traditional lands were recognized for the first time by the Supreme Court of Canada in the 2014 Tsilhqot'in decision. The real entitlement framework is constantly being adjusted and readjusted in relation to the balance of forces at play in struggles among social groups.

Yet from the time the first millennials were born, social rights and democratic control over the economy have been shrinking. I'll look at reasons why things have been changing since the 1970s in greater detail in the following chapters. The point here is that shrinking social rights encourage people to expect less outside the market, a development that's especially debilitating to people already disentitled by systems of racial, gender, and class inequality.

As entitlements to having needs met contract, people who fail to lower their expectations in accordance with the new normal can more easily appear to be selfish, harboring inflated ideas about what they deserve. The focus groups with students on campus confirm that some millennials have lowered their expectations. However, others are contributing to campaigns against the new normal, pressing for the expansion of what Chapter 2 defines as **democratic entitlements**. At work, on campus, and with respect to the natural environment there are counterflows to the forces of millennial disentitlement.

The following chapters examine these struggles in the Global North, the heart of the so-called entitlement epidemic. They touch on stories in different contexts: from low-income neighborhoods to university campuses to retail floors to Indigenous blockades to toxic shorelines and beyond.[3] At the same time as each chapter tells of powerful forces of dispossession, it also tells a counter-narrative about ongoing resistance driven by the belief that another world is possible, and the grueling work of bringing that world into being.

---

3 For a discussion of my research process, including reflections on my personal relationship to the millennial generation, see the Appendix: A Note on Methodology.

Chapter 2 argues that not all entitlement claims are the same and lays out a framework for distinguishing between different forms of deservingness. It compares the democratic entitlement claims of the contemporary Black Lives Matter movement to the **oppressive entitlement** claims of people and institutions who have embraced racial inequality throughout American history. Democratic entitlements involve feelings of deservingness and institutions that challenge inequality and aid the flourishing of collective self-government. Oppressive entitlements involve feelings of deservingness and institutions that embed inequality deeper into the social fabric.

Chapter 3 focuses on the myth of the age of entitlement at work. It contrasts familiar depictions of the lazy, entitled millennial worker to the reality of millennial disentitlement in "the precarious work society" (Wilson and Ebert 2013, 264). Employment arrangements in the "gig" economy of the millennial era are increasingly about unpaid internships; zero-hours contracts; and part-time, short-term jobs for poverty wages and no benefits. The chapter concludes by examining recent partial victories of workers demanding better treatment and a fairer share of the wealth they produce. The Fight for $15 campaign shows that the real entitlement framework can be transformed through mass mobilization from below. The activism of that campaign raises questions of what workers ought to be entitled to more broadly—not only in exchange for paid employment, but in all areas of our laboring lives.

Chapter 4 focuses on the myth of the age of entitlement on campus. It challenges recent warnings about the "coddling" of millennial college and university students (Lukianoff and Haidt 2015), and the notion that Gen Y suffers from "academic entitlement" (Boesveld 2014). In fact, policy changes designed to prepare students for lives as neoliberal workers and citizens disentitle Gen Y students in various ways. At the same time as higher education has become central to the millennial condition, student debt is skyrocketing, the learning process is being dehumanized, and campus-specific versions of the age of entitlement myth are undercutting student movements for greater equity. Yet there's also been a resurgence of student struggles for democratic entitlement. The 2012 Quebec student strike, campaigns against anti-black racism at the University of Missouri and Yale, and feminist struggles against gendered violence on campus point toward paths of postsecondary transformation in the name of genuine democracy and equity.

In Chapter 5, the myth of the age of entitlement collapses in the face of the ecological crisis. The chapter focuses on the experiences of teenagers in southern Louisiana who grew up in the aftermath of a massive oil spill in 2010. Their stories illustrate the ways climate change and other human-made environmental problems are disentitling millennials of the bases of life and hope in a sustainable future for themselves and their children. At the same time, millennials in South Lafourche are caught between wanting ecological sustainability yet depending on the success of the fossil fuel industry for their own economic security. The chapter concludes by reflecting on the ways in which new environmental movements devoted to meeting both economic and ecological needs offer visions of what a future era of expanding democratic entitlement must involve.

Chapter 6, the concluding chapter, addresses two questions: (1) How is it that an age of *dis*entitlement has become widely represented as its opposite? And (2) What do the case studies discussed throughout the book contribute to broader debates about democracy, environmental health, and social justice in the twenty-first century? I argue that in the absence of sustained mass movements for democratic entitlements, the decades-long context of attacks on social rights and increasing employer power make it easier to portray all claims of deservingness-from-below as excessive. Raising democracy to new heights and addressing the problem of inequality will involve the emergence and growth of new movements dedicated to satisfying needs regardless of the ability to pay, including the need for environmental justice. These movements will embody the maximalist demand chanted by coalitions of workers and students demonstrating for full control over social wealth in Italy in the 1970s: "Allt åt Alla!" Everything for everybody! (Katsiaficas 2006).

RAISING EXPECTATIONS

This book challenges the idea that we're plagued by an entitlement epidemic and that Generation Y is the most afflicted and most dangerously contagious carrier of the disease. The age of entitlement myth leaves out the politics of entitlement in debates about what millennials deserve. When the politics of entitlement are left out of debate, all sides end up smuggling in all sorts of unstated assumptions about what is "normal" or "excessive" to expect, and about who deserves to feel what. I want to refocus the discussion squarely on how these sorts of debates play out in actual social struggles and show why they're relevant not only to the situation of millennials but to the future of freedom, equality, and ecological health.

I wrote the book amid expressions of mass anger at politics-as-usual reaching heights not seen in my lifetime. Anti-establishment sentiment has given rise to political alternatives on both the right and left of the political spectrum that were outside the sphere of legitimate controversy not very long ago. Chapter 6 compares the similarly radical—albeit radically different—entitlement claims declared in the 2016 presidential campaigns of socialist Bernie Sanders and conservative Donald Trump. It's in the current context of social upheaval that debates over the age of entitlement matter most. What's at stake isn't just defining a term or coming to the right answer about whether millennials are bratty or not. What's at stake are the structures that will shape young people's futures.

Many young people are deeply anxious about their future. The transition from childhood to adulthood is always stressful. But the political, economic, and ecological crises that shape life in the twenty-first century place unique pressures on Gen Y's coming of age. There are trends and trajectories, pathways of possibility, that give clues about what's more or less likely to happen next. Yet there remains openness to what comes next, even when things appear settled. Speaking now directly to millennial readers, and readers of the generation to follow: *What your future looks like is still very much in play.* Whether the future ends up being more of the same or whether new variations in the real entitlement framework are to come depends on your historical agency—your ability to make history.

CHAPTER TWO

DEMOCRATIC AND OPPRESSIVE ENTITLEMENTS

MEANING IT

In 2012, a US-based consulting agency called the Aspen Group (2012) declared that Generation Y suffers from an intense "sense of entitlement." In a report called "Narcissistic and Entitled to Everything!" an Aspen Group therapist likens this trait to a voice in the millennial's head that repeats "I want it now! Now! I have to have it right now!" The report warns that members of Gen Y "feel entitled to their lifestyles, no matter how self-destructive," and that the millennial will "refuse to take responsibility when he makes a mistake."

In everyday conversations, it's usually clear what people mean when they talk about "a sense of entitlement." The common sense use of the term calls to mind images of people who think they're more deserving than everyone else. You could probably find examples of entitled young people in your own social circles without too much trouble. But what we mean exactly when we talk about *being entitled* or having a sense of entitlement needs fuller consideration. In the myth of the age of entitlement articulated by the Aspen Group, these terms have been used not just to characterize but to disparage a whole generation of young people. It's important to ensure we understand what we're talking about, and whether we're satisfied with the familiar story.

This chapter addresses the problem of the slippery meaning of the concept of entitlement. My concern is not that the word has been used "improperly" in the way that vexes English teachers. My concern is that the work it does within the age of entitlement myth shuts down the possibility that, in some situations, expecting more than what the status quo offers might actually be a positive thing. As the myth of the age of entitlement becomes part of the common sense concerning Generation Y, it becomes easier to dismiss any expectation that exceeds what's already on offer as an example of the entitlement epidemic. There can appear to be no difference between the millennial job applicant on *30 Rock* who says he's "not interested in the job unless I'm going to be constantly praised" (in Lyall 2016) and members of Gen Y demanding higher wages, student debt forgiveness, citizenship rights, or an end to offshore drilling. It all gets lumped into just so much more whining from spoiled, entitled millennials.

The thing is that not all expectations are identical. Senses of entitlement and legal entitlements reflect and restrict different locations in society and the access to power they afford. There is a politics of entitlement.

This chapter contributes to debates about who deserves access to what resources, and who is entitled to feel what, by comparing what I call *democratic entitlements* and *oppressive entitlements*. Democratic entitlements involve forms of deservingness that challenge inequality by establishing values and practices that strengthen the basis of collective self-governance in all areas of life. Oppressive entitlements involve forms of deservingness that ensure the privilege of some groups and the subordination of others in keeping with existing systems of inequality, such as sexism, white supremacy, and the exploitation of employees.

Distinguishing between different forms of entitlement can help move beyond the limited dominant frameworks for analyzing millennial challenges and opportunities. Greater conceptual precision in debates over millennial entitlement makes it easier to see the high stakes involved in these discussions. The question of whether millennials are especially entitled or not isn't the only thing on the line. Different visions of society are being promoted and attacked in these debates. The myth of the age of entitlement promotes a future of expanding market rule, in which people's needs and desires are met exclusively through consumer transactions. An alternative vision of the future imagines expanding social rights and democratic control over social and economic decisions. A new era of democracy and social justice will see millennials more collectively entitled to having more needs met and the necessary conditions for well-being accessible to everyone.

BLACK LIVES MATTER

Just after noon on 9 August 2014, an 18-year-old black man named Michael Brown was shot and killed by a white police officer in Ferguson, Missouri, a suburb of St. Louis. Brown was unarmed when he was gunned down by Officer Darren Wilson. According to eye-witness Dorian Johnson, Brown's hands were in the air when Wilson fired the lethal bullets. "Michael's body jerks as if he was hit," said Tiffany Mitchell, another eyewitness, "then he put his hands up." At this point, reported Johnson, Brown yelled, "I don't have a gun, stop shooting!" (in Robles and Bosman 2014). Officer Wilson shot Brown four times in the right arm and twice in the head. For the next four hours, Brown's dead body lay in the middle of the street.

Special attention was drawn to Ferguson because Brown's killing happened amid growing movements to stop violence against young black men. Two years before Wilson killed Brown, an unarmed young black man named Trayvon Martin was shot to death by George Zimmerman in a small Florida community. At the time he was killed, Martin was returning to his father's fiancée's home after buying candy and soda at the corner store. Zimmerman, a Latino community-watch volunteer, didn't like the look of Martin, who was wearing a hoodie and walking through the neighborhood in the rain. Seventeen-year-old Martin ran from the SUV that Zimmerman trailed him with, fleeing toward the safety of his home. He was shot to death by Zimmerman before reaching the house. On 13 July 2013 Zimmerman was declared not guilty of second-degree murder and left court a free man. The stories of Brown and Martin attracted unprecedentedly expansive media coverage; however, as political scientist Michael Hanchard (2015) wrote, violence against black people by police and other authorities is "unfortunately nothing new. [...] These incidents are all too common in black and brown communities in various parts of the world."

Soon after Trayvon Martin's killer went unpunished, a small group of queer women-of-color activists began using the hashtag #BlackLivesMatter. They launched the phrase to raise awareness about the fact that violence against black people is a routine part of American society and to call special attention to the daily harm done to queer black women. In the words of Alicia Garza (2014), one of the first to use the slogan, "Black Lives Matter is an ideological and political intervention in a world where Black lives are systematically and intentionally targeted for demise. It is an affirmation of Black folks' contributions to this society, our humanity, and our resilience in the face of deadly oppression."

As Professor Hanchard (2015) wrote in the *Huffington Post*, "The killing of unarmed black men is part of a larger problem of the legacies of racial regimes in societies where disproportionately high levels of unemployment and incarceration rates, poor education, spatial segregation and capricious doses of state violence, structure the conditions of marginality which makes violence against these populations not only plausible, but banal." Envisioning the kind of fundamental social transformation that would replace today's disproportionately high levels of black poverty, black prisoners, and black people without citizenship protection, #BlackLivesMatter declared that black people deserve to have "our basic human rights and dignity" recognized. The slogan asserted that black communities are entitled to better than the status quo.

Immediately after hearing the words Black Lives Matter, I was reminded of a lecture delivered at Ryerson University a few years before the killing of Michael Brown. American historian Komozi Woodard (2011) spoke in Toronto about the deep historical roots of black liberation movements in the United States. In his analysis of the different factors that ended legalized slavery, Woodard emphasized the centrality of what he called "a collective sense of entitlement to a better life" among African American slaves.

In contrast to official histories and Hollywood treatments of the emancipation era, which focus on singular actions of Great (usually white) Men, such as Abraham Lincoln, Woodard argued that understanding advances in black freedom requires recognizing the inexhaustible feelings of deservingness that were nurtured and shared throughout slave communities. Slaves organized attacks on their captors, built complex escape routes across thousands of miles, took up arms against the Confederate Army in the Civil War, worked with free blacks in nonslave states to press politicians to advocate abolition. Woodard expressed wonderment at the fact that not even the most brutal systematic abuse and daily indignities meted out by the slave-owning class and its supporters were able to break African American slaves' will to resist, their insistence that they were entitled to freedom and justice.

Throughout the fall of 2014, as tens of thousands of Black Lives Matter demonstrators marched through dozens of cities to protest racist violence, they appeared to be moved by something like the *collective sense of entitlement* described by Woodard. In an interview with the *New York Times Magazine*, a prominent activist stated the bare minimum of what the movement is seeking to change: "Our demand is simple. Stop killing us." Yet, as the Black Lives Matter (2016) website explains, this is but the essential starting point for activists' expansive vision of black liberation: "When we say Black Lives Matter, we are broadening the conversation around state violence to include all of the ways in which Black people are intentionally left powerless at the hands of the state." Black Lives Matter envisions an end not only to the unjust killing of black people, but to the poverty and criminalization of black communities that constantly erodes black livelihoods and undercuts black power. Sabaah Jordan, a recent graduate of Columbia University, drew these connections while marching in a Black Lives Matter rally in New York:

> We're building a movement. We believe that we can live in a better world. [...] We're in a world where it's difficult to find a job, it's difficult to pay off student loans—everything is very difficult. And so, it forces you to ask questions: Why is it like this? And then, when you see people being killed in the street and police officers not being held accountable, that's just one more thing that tells you that something is really, really wrong and that if we don't do anything about

it, that this is the world that we're going to inherit as adults.
It's hard to think about having children as a black woman in
this world right now. And so, that's where I'm coming from.
(In Goodman 2014)

In its "refusal to accept politics as they stand" (Wright 2015),
the Black Lives Matter movement exhibits aspects of the sense of
entitlement maligned in the age of entitlement myth. The movement expects exceptional treatment of groups suffering from racist
oppression. The self-conception of Black Lives Matter activists is far
more favorable than the ways in which black people in general and
the movement in particular tend to be seen and represented in mainstream political and pop culture. The movement claims black people
deserve resources and supports on account of their very existence,
not as payment for services rendered or reward for good behavior.
It encourages black people to refuse the norm, to raise their expectations. Certainly critics of Black Lives Matter portray it as being
overly entitled.[4]

But the fact that Black Lives Matter is driven by and cultivates
a sense of entitlement is part of its strength as a movement for social justice. The history of black liberation struggles in the United
States is a history of feeling entitled to self-determination, dignity,
and essential resources and fighting to turn the feeling into reality.
Black Lives Matter models both a collective sense of and movement
for *democratic entitlement*.

---

4 While online comment sections are not known for being sources of
great insight, the patterns in them can shed light on relevant, even if offensive, threads in public discussion. In this respect, it's relevant that following the January 2015 posting "State of the Black Union" on the Black Lives
Matter website, two different commenters attacked the movement using the
language of entitlement. The first writes, "Several of your demands regard
the need for supplied housing or shelter, food, and more. What gives you the
right or entitlement to these when other Americans do not have them?" The
second writes, "Why don't you do what every other American has done and
WORK for the things you feel you are entitled to. But you are entitled to it ...
if you earn it." The comments have since been taken down.

DEMOCRATIC ENTITLEMENTS

There are three key features that distinguish democratic entitlements from the harmful qualities typically associated with the term. First, they involve forms of deservingness that challenge existing systems of inequality and press toward greater political and economic equity. Examples of democratic entitlement in action include anti-poverty movements fighting against inequalities of wealth, Indigenous struggles to dismantle colonialism, and campaigns led by disabled people rooted in a sense of deserving no less access than able-bodied people.

It was a radical sense of democratic entitlement that drove the "Wages for Housework" campaign of the 1970s. Feminist activists called attention to the unequal value attributed to domestic work, traditionally done by women, compared to the sort of paid work traditionally done by male breadwinners. Not only is domestic work treated as less important than professional work, but housework is literally unpaid. Of course, domestic work is no less crucial to the reproduction of society than work in offices or factories. In the name of gender equity, the Wages for Housework campaign demanded women be paid for their essential domestic labor. Activists knew they would be called delusional and entitled, accused of expecting too much. That is why they wrote, "It is not for us to put limits on our power, it is not for us to measure our value. It is only for us to organize a struggle to get all of what we want, for us all, and on our terms" (in Weeks 2011, 132). One Wages for Housework pamphlet read: "WE WANT IT IN CASH, RETROACTIVE AND IMMEDIATELY, AND WE WANT ALL OF IT" (135).

In the words of political theorist Kathi Weeks (2011, 133), Wages for Housework "was not just a goal but also a movement, a process of becoming the kind of people who—or, rather, the kind of collectivities that—needed, wanted, and *felt entitled* to a wage for their contributions" (emphasis added). The ultimate aim of the movement was an end to gender inequality and the poverty faced by people prevented from accessing livable wages for whatever reason. The material demand—wages for housework—was foundational to but not exhaustive of the broader political vision: full equity and collective self-government in all areas of life.

Second, democratic entitlements strengthen collective capacities to govern ourselves. The more equitably that decision-making power and resources are shared, the greater chance everyone will have to live flourishing lives. This is the promise of democracy. Black Americans fighting for full citizenship rights in the 1950s and 1960s were called uppity and unrealistic. Opponents of the civil rights movement said black people should accept their normal place in the social order. Feeling entitled to full political participation, people of color refused to lower their expectations and fought for collective self-determination.

From across the spectrum of black liberation movements in the civil rights period, every iconic image of anti-racist resistance reflects a surging sense of entitlement to full democratic rights. Rosa Parks refusing to give up her seat on the bus; Martin Luther King leading crowds across the Selma bridge; Black Panthers feeding poor children in community-run breakfast programs (and carrying guns into the California legislature to protest police violence); Malcolm X talking with Fidel Castro of Cuba, Abdel Nasser of Egypt, and other leaders of "the Third World project," who were themselves part of movements driven by mass senses of entitlement among people in "the darker nations" for decolonization (Prashad 2007). At the time, many American officials condemned the civil rights movement. Today there's no question that its successes strengthened democracy in America. The transformation was urged on by swelling senses of democratic entitlement.

Democracies are based on the principle of *rule by the people*. While the official political system is one place where new experiments in popular participation might help to deepen democracy, there are other institutions, including schools and workplaces, in which members currently excluded from key decision-making roles have long felt entitled to greater authority over their own working conditions. For example, student movements of the 1960s and 1970s declared that students deserved to run their schools. In May 1968, thousands of students in Paris took over their campuses, occupying buildings and running the institutions using techniques of mass participatory democracy. The democratic vision of the students was multidimensional. It included student control of the universities, an end to French imperialism, and better wages and working conditions for factory workers. These students, too, were called spoiled and entitled; but their supporters, such as the philosopher Herbert Marcuse (1969, 44) saw in the student movement's radical vision of solidarity and democracy "the ferment of hope ... and the real possibility of a free society."

In his study of the 1960s and 1970s student movements, sociologist George Katsiaficas (1987, 7) refers to "the eros effect" in explaining how collective senses of democratic entitlement can surge and spread suddenly during moments of mass movement mobilization. Eros is the Roman god of love. Katsiaficas argues that unique types of love are unleashed when people experience the horizons of possibility expanding as a result of their own activism. "Such periods of the *eros* effect witness the basic assumptions and values of a social order," such as hierarchy and nationalism, "being challenged in theory and practice by new human standards. The capacity of millions of people to see beyond the social reality of their day—to imagine a better world and fight for it—demonstrates a human characteristic (the *eros* effect) which may be said to transcend time and space" (ibid.)

At a Black Lives Matter demonstration in New York City, Kayesha shook her head explaining what the protest meant to her: "It's amazing. It's empowering. I've never seen anything like this. This is my first protest in this magnitude. And I just—I feel so proud. I'm elated. I feel strong. I feel empowered. And I'm just grateful to be a part of changing history" (in Goodman 2014). A robust sense among less powerful people that they deserve more fulsome, more meaningful participation in the decision-making processes that affect their lives has fueled every democratic advance in history.

Finally, democratic entitlements involve satisfying human needs to help people live flourishing lives and further the collective development of human potential. Policies and programs designed to meet people's needs for health care, housing, food, transportation, and ecological sustainability tend to be fed by currents of democratic entitlement. As Black Lives Matter activists have explained, only when black communities are free both from racist violence and from barriers preventing them from satisfying economic needs will it become possible to move toward true racial justice.

Borrowing language from economics professor Michael Lebowitz (2010, 44), who is himself borrowing from the nineteenth-century critical political economist Karl Marx, democratic entitlements are necessary for "the production of rich human beings." Lebowitz does not mean rich in the sense of owning multiple yachts and luxury watches. Rich, in Lebowitz's sense, is about the unique value created by human cooperation under conditions in which the work we do at home, on the job, and in our communities is organized to contribute to the well-being of all while, at the same time, we all benefit more equitably from the work of everyone else. Lebowitz calls this vision of "worker and community management" of our productive activity "the solidarian society," a radically democratic political–economic alternative oriented toward meeting human needs (65).

This might sound utopian. Indeed it is, if what's being evoked by the term *utopia* is the imagined character of such a society at this moment, the *nowhereness* of it.[5] It definitely sounds a lot like novelist and cultural critic Benjamin Kunkel's (2014, 2) vision of a more democratic alternative, and Kunkel's book is called *Utopia or Bust*. His vision includes "public ownership of important economic and financial institutions" operating in the service of democracy and social equality. As political theorist Kathi Weeks (2011, 193) argues, "utopian thinking" has long been part of political projects "inspired by the desire for and will to new and better forms of life." Historian Robin D.G. Kelley (2002) writes of the unique power of the "freedom dreams" that fuel "the black radical imagination" in the face of centuries of oppression.

Anti-slavery struggles in mid-nineteenth-century America were utopian in that they were otherworldly, oriented toward a time not yet come. Elements of what Weeks (2011, 235) calls "utopian hope" fuel Black Lives Matter organizing; but in her view, an audacious anti-racist vision is essential to democratic transformation. Weeks is not worried that democratic movements are overly ambitious; her concern is that "we do not want enough." By envisioning and working toward meeting human needs, especially the needs of marginalized groups, democratic entitlements strengthen the basis on which social justice might be raised to new heights.

---

5 In Thomas More's classic book *Utopia*, published in 1516, the name of the fictional land was Erehwon ("nowhere" spelled backward).

By itself, the concept of democratic entitlements neither identifies which campaigns, policies, and shared feelings of deservingness "count" as democratic, nor does it provide an instruction manual for making democracy work. Yet there is no need to produce an exhaustive list of democratic entitlements to clarify where the democratic currents are in competing visions of deservingness. These currents are at risk of being delegitimized by the age of entitlement myth, which opposes all claims for enhanced deservingness. We need language capable of reflecting the fact that not all forms of entitlement serve the same political ends. As the next section shows, certain visions of deservingness are anti-democratic.

THE NEW JIM CROW

In the mid-1850s, Dred Scott was an African American slave living in the state of Missouri. The laws of that state entitled John Sanford, a white man, to own Scott and his family. Scott claimed that he was entitled to freedom and sued Sanford for "battery and wrongful imprisonment" (Finkelman 2006, 24). Scott's legal case was based on the fact that years earlier, his previous master (Dr. John Emerson) had moved him to jurisdictions in which slavery was banned (Illinois and Wisconsin). Scott argued that while living in free states he had become officially free. Having gained that status once, it could not be taken from him again. Despite Scott's unique circumstances, his case offered the court a chance to set wide-reaching precedents over freedom claims of escaped slaves.

In 1857, the Supreme Court of the United States ruled against Scott and against black rights more broadly. Chief justice of the Supreme Court, Roger Brooke Taney, wrote in his decision that "the right of property in a slave is distinctly and expressly affirmed in the Constitution" (in Finkelman 2006, 42). Even a slave who had been moved by his owner from a slave state to a free state "was not entitled to his freedom" (Urofsky 2016). Chief Justice Taney wrote that blacks were "an inferior class of beings ... so far inferior, that they had no rights which the white man was bound to respect" (Finkelman 2006, 38). When the ruling came down it was opposed by anti-slavery activists, but "it was possible to find numerous supporters of Taney's reasoning, analysis, and conclusions. Southerners generally applauded the decision, and many were ecstatic over it" (5).

In the century between the abolition of legal slavery (in 1865) and the victory of full citizenship rights for African Americans (in the 1960s), the white population in the United States continued to be entitled to all sorts of privileges denied the black population. In the era of formal segregation referred to as the Jim Crow period,[6] black people were banned from participating in most of the economic, cultural, and political spaces of white society, including white schools, railcars, and lunch counters (see National Park Service 2016). In Georgia, black barbers were legally barred from serving white women or girls. In Mississippi, it was an offense punishable by jail to write or distribute ideas "in favor of social equality or of intermarriage between whites and negroes." In Alabama, the governor personally tried to prevent Arthurine Lucy, a black student, from enrolling at one of the state's white-only universities. Thousands of black men and women were beaten and lynched (illegally killed by a crowd, often publicly) without the white aggressors facing trial or punishment.

The racist legal mechanisms and political symbolism structuring the real entitlement framework of the Jim Crow period were different than they had been before 1865. However, the overarching framework of who is entitled to what and entitled to feel what continued to reflect and reproduce white supremacy and the dispossession of black communities. American sociologist C. Wright Mills (1997, 269) defined white supremacy as

> a political, economic, and cultural system in which whites overwhelmingly control power and material resources, conscious and unconscious ideas of white superiority and entitlement are widespread, and relations of white dominance and non-white subordination are daily reenacted across a broad array of institutions and social settings.

---

6 The name refers to a racist stage show by a white performer in "blackface" in the 1830s.

Critical race theorist bell hooks (1988) says that the concept of white supremacy is essential because it names the special advantages and authority granted to white people as the source of racial inequality.

Ohio State University law professor Michelle Alexander (2010) argues that in the post-1960s civil rights era, despite important gains won by black Americans, white supremacy in the United States continues to be supported by various institutions, none less important than the system of mass incarceration. In her book *The New Jim Crow*, Alexander writes, "We have not ended racial caste in America; we have merely redesigned it" (2). The end of the Jim Crow period meant that legal discrimination on the basis of race could no longer ensure white supremacy. This also made it much more difficult to use overtly racist language and reasoning to maintain white privilege. "In the era of colorblindness," writes Alexander,

> it is no longer socially permissible to use race, explicitly, as a justification for discrimination, exclusion, and social contempt. So we don't. Rather than rely on race, we use our criminal justice system, to label people of color "criminals" and then engage in all the practices we supposedly left behind. Today it is perfectly legal to discriminate against criminals in nearly all the ways that it was once legal to discriminate against African Americans. Once you're labeled a felon, the old forms of discrimination—employment discrimination, housing discrimination, denial of the right to vote, denial of educational opportunity, denial of food stamps and of public benefits, and exclusion from jury service—are suddenly legal. (ibid.)

Incarceration rates in the United States have exploded since the end of Jim Crow. In 1970, fewer than 100 of every 100,000 Americans were locked up; today, the rate is more than 500 in 100,000 (Prison Policy Initiative 2016). A hugely disproportionate number of the more than 2 million men and women locked in cages in the United States are people of color (US Government 2015). African Americans make up around 12 percent of the US population but comprise close to

38 percent of the prison population. Scholar and activist Angela Davis (2003, 94–5) notes that "the incarcerated population is approaching the proportion of black prisoners to white during the era of the southern convict lease and county chain gang systems" of the Jim Crow period.

As Alexander, Davis, and other critical legal scholars argue, this unequal outcome is not the result of communities of color being "more" criminal. It is the result of an unequal framework of who is entitled to what that criminalizes specific types of behavior (such as possession of small amounts of drugs) and not others (such as ordering a war responsible for killing thousands of civilians in Iraq). This framework aggressively polices certain activities in poor black communities (such as drug possession) while allowing those same activities to go unpoliced within wealthier white communities. "White Americans are more likely than black Americans to have used most kinds of illegal drugs, including cocaine, marijuana and LSD. Yet blacks are far more likely to go to prison for drug offenses" (Knafo 2013).

Critical race scholars help see the challenges of black communities within a whole system of social relations that tend to benefit white people through the subordination of black people. In so doing, they avoid the mistake of treating social trends as isolated phenomena. Without suggesting there is a one-to-one relationship between the success of Person Y and the hardships of Person X, this critical perspective interprets trends as being mutually constitutive. By emphasizing the interconnectedness of social trends, the relational approach casts doubt on the age of entitlement narrative for treating era-of-birth as the primary trait of millennials. To the extent that generational traits exist, they cannot be separated from relationships that structure social life running along lines of economic class, gender, or race. A relational approach is essential to the concept of oppressive entitlement.

OPPRESSIVE ENTITLEMENTS

In a Pulitzer Prize–winning book-length letter to his son, journalist and public intellectual Ta-Nehisi Coates (2015) explains that the severe racial inequalities of the twenty-first century didn't grow naturally or by chance. The disproportionate wealth and power of white America, from Independence to today, has been maintained through violence against black bodies. Borrowing a phrase from writer James Baldwin, Coates writes, "the elevation of the belief in being white"—the construction of whiteness as the dominant social identity—"was not achieved through wine tastings and ice cream socials,"

> but rather through the pillaging of life, liberty, labor, and land; through the flaying of backs; the chaining of limbs; the strangling of dissidents; the destruction of families; the rape of mothers; the sale of children; and various other acts meant, first and foremost, to deny you and me the right to secure and govern our own bodies. (8)

Writing to his teenage son not long after the killings of Trayvon Martin, Michael Brown, Tamir Rice, and dozens of other young black men and women, Coates links the special entitlements of white America—the privilege of what he calls living "the Dream"—to the disposability of black people. "There is no them without you," he says to his son; "and without the right to break you they must necessarily fall from the mountain, lose their divinity, and tumble out of the Dream" (105). In language more poetic and provocative than academics tend to use, Coates articulates a truism of critical sociology: namely, that privilege and oppression form two parts of a larger social whole; they cannot be explained in isolation.

Entitlement is oppressive when one or more of three ingredients are in the mix. First, currents of oppressive entitlement are reproduced by feelings of deservingness or institutional supports rooted in social hierarchies. These patterns are always harmful, but they are not always outwardly violent. For example, in a study of how students develop self-identity at arts-based high schools, sociologists Ruben Gaztambide-Fernandez, Kate Cairns (who, yes, is my sister), and Chandni Desai (2013) show that oppressive entitlements operate even in places that prize hard work. They conclude that students whose identity is formed through associations with their elite school tend to conceive of themselves as deserving the special status and enhanced opportunities afforded to them.

The researchers acknowledge the positive aspects of developing a sense of deservingness and collective identity. The problem with the particular sense of entitlement encouraged through elite education is that its very existence requires that most people are excluded from its special advantages. The "positive feelings" students expressed about helping disadvantaged communities were not rooted in commitment to equality and democracy but to feelings of superiority over others, developed in relation to their school's elite status. The feelings of entitlement fostered by an elite education are oppressive because they suggest that some groups of people are deserving of special privileges not available to others.

At a global scale, the US government is officially committed to due process before the law. However, in the real entitlement framework governing geopolitics, the United States regularly demonstrates that it is entitled to kill people without charge or trial in other parts of the world. Political analyst and MIT professor Noam Chomsky (2015) has said that the US government appears to feel "entitled to resort to violence at will." Defenders of the US drone program say that the government's extrajudicial killings are justified because the people being put to death are terrorists. This does not explain why the US government faces no trial, no punishment, no form of accountability for the drone killing of civilians not suspected of terrorism, which the Bureau of Investigative Journalism (2016) estimates to be as high as 966 people in Pakistan alone (between 2004 and 2015), including up to 207 children. Yet even if the people being assassinated in every case were in fact murderers themselves (which they're not), the government's self-granted right to kill outside of the legal process it imposes on all others clearly constitutes a form of entitlement. It's a case of oppressive entitlement because it reflects and reproduces an unequal geopolitical order—one in which the enormous power of the United States depends on other countries not being entitled to act in the same ways.

Second, currents of oppressive entitlement are strengthened through institutions and feelings that treat human beings exclusively as individuals. Doing so denies the fact that we are also social beings who, at present, live in complex societies built on interdependence and structured around severe group-based inequalities. Failing to recognize the social character of the human condition weakens our collective capacity to solve social problems and restricts the full development of individuals and communities (see Ferguson and McNally 2015; Marx 1844). Oppressive dynamics tend to be at play whenever an individual claims (or assumes himself to be) so singularly knowledgeable or skilled that he is entitled to riches or status granting him control over others. Political and economic institutions that treat people exclusively as individuals, making it impossible to attend to our social condition, similarly facilitate and encourage oppressive entitlements.

The characterization of Western economies as being organized by the principle of meritocracy is a good example of how the denial of our social character can help legitimize oppressive entitlements right out in the open. The term *meritocracy* refers to a system in which rewards and social status are distributed according to merit. As Nicole Aschoff (2015, 102) observes in her study of the myths of modern capitalism, "The American Dream is premised on the assumption that if you work hard economic opportunity will present itself and financial stability will follow." The dream continues to appeal to large sections of Gen Y: A 2014 Reason-Rupe poll reported that 57 percent of millennials said they "prefer a society where wealth is distributed according to one's achievement" (as opposed to "an economically egalitarian society where the income gap between rich and poor is small regardless of achievement") (Ekins 2014, 72).

In a properly functioning meritocracy, anyone who's smart and works hard and devotes herself to years of training can rise to the heights of her chosen field. This reasoning is used to justify why corporate leaders like Microsoft CEO Bill Gates deserve the high salaries and prestige that goes along with their place at the top: supposedly, they got there on account of their merits. On the flip side, when the contemporary economy is viewed as a meritocracy, unemployed people, homeless people, and people who don't like their jobs have got no one to blame but themselves. Assuming that we live in a meritocracy supports a theory of entitlement that basically says "if you've got it, you deserve it."

Crude as that sounds, it's precisely this assumption that undergirds the late American philosopher Robert Nozick's (1974) "theory of entitlement." Nozick's entitlement theory is concerned with the big philosophical questions of what people are entitled to own and possess and what they are entitled to share (or, more important to Nozick, what they are entitled *not* to share). More concretely, he's speaking to debates about whether the state has the right or responsibility to support people in need through social programs funded through higher taxes on wealthy people and corporations. In Nozick's language, he's reflecting on the "justice" of "transferring shares" or "the holdings" of some individuals to others.

Nozick argues that it is unjust in every instance for the state or another body of collective governance to redistribute "shares," no matter how noble or fair it seems. The collective redistribution of wealth is unjust because it interferes with the individual's entitlements to do what he likes with what he has. In Nozick's philosophy, taxes are theft. Welfare programs are nothing other than undeserving poor people (and all poor people are undeserving) stealing from those who have money. If a person has accumulated money, he is entitled to do what he wants with it.

Nozick's theory attempts to justify oppressive entitlements by denying the social character of all goods and services. Nozick treats the wealth accumulated by the richest individuals, corporations, and governments around us today as though it were rightfully theirs because they were its original producers. This grossly misrepresents history. It only partially accounts for what goes into the production of goods and services. And it erases the uneven systems of privilege and oppression that structure people's chances to succeed.

As one critic writes in the philosophy journal *Inquiry*, "Since Nozick's argument fails to show how individuals can acquire full entitlement in the first place, he has not given reasons" for interpreting all redistribution of wealth as a form of injustice (O'Neill 2008, 480). An honest account of history reveals that all wealth and power within the United States and Canada is founded on the violent dispossession of the Indigenous peoples of North America. The riches of Europe's ruling classes today were raised through the plundering of Africa. Sociologist David Calnitsky puts it this way:

> Bill Gates would have no wealth at all were it not for the
> society that he happened to have been born into, were

it not for the benefits conferred onto him from living in that society. Had he been born on a desert island he would not have had the roads, the teachers, not to mention the technologies, the language, that made his earnings possible, that he tapped into free of charge. His output is only possible on the basis of the prior developments of a society and an economy in which he was plopped into. (Personal communication)

A sense of entitlement is oppressive when it erases history to legitimize current power imbalances.

Nozick is also distorting reality when he suggests that everyone is entitled to the same life chances. If they were, writes Aschoff (2015, 103), "we should see the effects of this in increased upward mobility and wealth created anew by new people in each generation rather than passed down and expanded from one generation to the next. The data do not demonstrate this upward mobility." In fact, as the French economist Thomas Piketty (2014) documents in his research on the past 400 years of wealth inequality, wealth has become *more* concentrated among privileged social groups in modern times. "The rich are getting richer and will in all likelihood—given the current relationship between returns on capital and economic growth—get even richer" (Aschoff 2015, 104). As *Wired* magazine notes, even in the millennial-dominated start-up scene of Silicon Valley, which "really wants to be a meritocracy [...] the people succeeding in tech have a pretty homogenous background" (Alba 2015). They're former senior executives of other major tech companies or people who have attended one of three schools: Stanford, Harvard, or the Massachusetts Institute of Technology. The story of the Self-Made Man is a fiction.

At the same time as we are individuals, we are also part of complex webs of work and ideas that tie us to other humans around the world, as well as to the physical and mental fruits produced by the labor of our species reaching back thousands of years. It can be difficult to see or feel these bonds of mutual dependence because our experiences of the world are highly mediated by a capitalist economy, in which society's key productive resources (and the wealth they produce) are owned and controlled by individuals and private corporations.

The social character of the wealth tapped by private owners is not recognized; nor is the wealth accumulated by private owners shared collectively, despite being dependent on collective action.

Everyday experiences under capitalism—on the job, in the market, and at play—tend to exaggerate our sense of individualness and obscure our deep dependence on others. Because Nozick's entitlement theory aligns with everyday experiences of life under capitalism, it takes critical thinking to reject a sense of entitlement in his tradition. But assuming his viewpoint means dismissing the webs of history and social forces responsible for contemporary riches, poverty, and other inequalities. Institutions and attitudes that justify uneven privileges in terms of the merits of individuals help reproduce relationships of oppression.

The third ingredient that makes entitlements oppressive is when they stunt the development of the conditions necessary for more fully and widely meeting human needs. There are heated scholarly debates about the difference between a want and a need, what counts as a *real* need, and whether needs change over time. The economist Michael Lebowitz (1977/78) argues that answers cannot be formulated in the abstract. It's futile to try to create a master list distinguishing needs from wants from whims, as though these phenomena exist independently from the goods and cultural values developed within a particular time and place.

Do you *need* a cell phone? You'd be unlikely to die without one. But if you didn't have a cell phone, could you find and hold down the job you're aiming for, maintain connections with friends and family, or navigate the city in anything like the manner that's now expected by employers, school administrators, and government officials, to say nothing of new friends? I didn't need a cell phone when I was an undergrad in the late 1990s. Lots of people had them, but they hadn't yet become an essential part of the social landscape. Twenty years later, as the social uses of technology have changed, needs have changed, too. Needs are produced in relation to available technologies, infrastructures, knowledges, and the expectations that emerge around them.

Lebowitz observes that human needs have never been so complex or varied as they are at this moment in history. Moreover, the human capacity to meet needs has never been stronger. There is more than enough wealth and technology available to satisfy the needs of everyone for access to food, water, medicine, transportation, and more (Oxfam Canada 2016). Yet millions of people struggle daily to satisfy even their most basic needs, while their fuller suite of needs is denied altogether. Guaranteeing a select group of people access to goods and services by restricting access to others constitutes an oppressive form of entitlement.

This was essentially the argument made by defenders of "net neutrality" that won landmark protections for Internet freedom in 2015. For years, the companies who own the transmission lines through which Internet traffic travels have been attempting to restrict access to their property to those willing and able to pay. Internet companies wanted to create different tiers of Internet access, restricting higher-speed connections to higher-paying customers (just as cable companies charge fees for different packages).

A broad-based movement calling for net neutrality mobilized behind the demand for maintaining equal access to Internet transmission. It included religious groups, labor unions, librarians, and the founders of the Internet. Three-quarters of a million Americans signed a petition in favor of net neutrality, and hackers protested restricting Internet service by disrupting service during specific periods. Media scholars Lawrence Lessig and Robert McChesney (2006) wrote an article in the *Washington Post* framing Internet access as a need in the modern economy and condemning Internet companies for attempting to profit by restricting access to it.

In this case, activists won. The oppressive nature of Internet companies' sense of deservingness to do whatever they wanted with the lines was ruled out of bounds. But a victory for the universal satisfaction of human needs against forces pressing to restrict needs being granted to specific groups is increasingly rare. Under today's real entitlement framework, there are significant challenges facing social movements pressing for the reorganization of social wealth to meet the rich needs of everyone.

The concept of oppressive entitlement aims to make it easier to see patterns not always observable on the surface of daily life. It is not a replacement for critical categories dealing with oppression, such as sexism, racism, or exploitation. It is an additional tool for thinking about the ways in which different forms of oppression interact and the processes through which one particular current in common sense— namely, the myth of the age of entitlement—helps reproduce and justify sexism, racism, and economic inequality in ways that are best understood in relation to one another.

THE CONTRADICTIONS OF DESERVINGNESS

Drawing distinctions between democratic and oppressive entitlements helps open up debates about the fairness of existing policies and attitudes governing who deserves what. The concepts facilitate more rigorous reflection on whether existing and proposed patterns of deservingness strengthen democracy and challenge inequality, or whether they consolidate social hierarchies, deepening and extending inequalities that privilege some by subordinating others. The myth of the age of entitlement frames the problem of excessive millennial deservingness within a single category: era-of-birth. While there are undoubtedly differences among generations, there are serious limits to what generational analysis can observe and explain. The concepts of democratic and oppressive entitlement allow questions of appropriate or excessive deservingness to be approached along multiple axes.

It is rare that a policy, movement, idea, or feeling is purely either democratic or oppressive. In reality, people's sense of deservingness and the legal entitlements upheld through political–economic institutions almost always involve tensions between democratic and oppressive currents. For example, as the next chapter explains, democratic entitlements expanded when the surging power of labor unions in the middle of the twentieth century won higher wages and stronger protections for working-class people. Yet the same economic changes that saw more and more (mostly male, white) workers earning enough money to support a family meant that women were expected to do all the essential but unpaid domestic labor, such as keeping house and raising children. Major labor unions that helped win historic gains for workers continued to be formally racially segregated. How do we respond when different projects of democratic entitlement contradict each other?

Community activists negotiate such tensions all the time. Immigrant rights groups demanding citizenship status for undocumented people work in coalition with Indigenous activists who reject the state's authority to grant citizenship altogether. Activists in the Global South fighting for greater shares of the wealth concentrated in the Global North do so at the same time as rejecting the ecologically harmful industries underpinning Northern power. The work of these activists demonstrates that the most honest and effective way forward will be messy. Contradictions need to be recognized and won't always be resolved fully at the level of ideas. They will be negotiated and reshaped through grassroots social movement organizing.

The case studies in the following three chapters illustrate where the currents of democratic and oppressive entitlements run through key areas of concern to Generation Y. These chapters do not draw up a comprehensive list of which people and institutions are democratic as opposed to which are oppressive. Instead, I seek to identify the key democratic and oppressive forces at play in different contexts, understand their main sources of strength and what opposes them, and explain how they interact with each other. My hope is for this book to provide a clearer view of the struggles that shape the real entitlement framework so that people are better equipped in their efforts to transform it.

As demonstrated in Chapter 1, democratic currents have weakened in the millennial era. The following chapters trace this trend in relation to growing oppressive currents. But this is only part of the story. I will have failed if by shining light on disentitling trends readers are left feeling overwhelmed by fear. There is reason for "hope without optimism," to borrow the phrase of cultural critic Terry Eagleton (2015). Viewing contemporary social problems with clear eyes, Eagleton dismisses the sort of "things are bound to get better" attitudes based on nothing more than faith; but he encourages hope where there are material reasons for believing that positive change is possible.

The grounds for hope today lie in movements for a new age of expanded democratic entitlements. This sort of activism is found in a range of areas: students campaigning for free tuition, Indigenous activists refusing to relinquish sovereignty, environmental activists championing alternatives to the fossil fuel economy that ensure ecological sustainability and economic security for working-class people. These movements provide clues about what a world rooted in greater democratic entitlement might look like and provide hope that such a world is possible. The following case studies examine struggles between forces of democratic and oppressive entitlements in various contexts. Chapter 3 kicks it off in the workplace, home to some of the loudest grumblings about millennial entitlement gone wild.

CHAPTER THREE

ZEROED DOWN: THE FLEXIBLE MILLENNIAL WORKER

HORROR SHOW

The 2015 season opener of *Saturday Night Live* (*SNL*) was hosted by popstar Miley Cyrus. At different points in the show, Cyrus danced suggestively in a poodle skirt, watched a friend fake a massive orgasm, and impersonated actor Hayley Mills. Cyrus also played a young office worker in a trailer for a spoof television series called "The Millennials." Ominous strings played in the background as a booming voice described the show as "a workplace drama unlike anything you've ever seen."

The trailer opened with a gray-haired boss gazing out an office window. A twentysomething shuffled into the room, texting and wearing an oversized floppy hat. Without looking at her boss (she was still texting), the young employee immediately demanded a promotion. "And I don't 'want' it," she whined, "I *deserve* it." Visibly taken aback, the boss asked how long she'd worked there. The millennial answered: "Three full days!"

Cyrus and her fellow Gen Y workers announced plans to travel through the south of France, texted constantly (pausing only to snap selfies), and asked for directions to "the nap room." In a voice fit for a slasher film promo, the narrator proclaimed, "The Millennials. A show that explores what no other dares to: beautiful twentysomethings trying to find the success and love they're entitled to."

For years before the *SNL* spoof aired, business analysts warned employers of a terrifying threat to corporate success: the rise of the millennial employee. And they weren't trying to be funny. The Money section of *US News* called millennial workers "needy ... entitled ... [and] disloyal" (Graves 2012). In the *Chicago Tribune*, human resource execs said that the millennial "sense of entitlement" makes running a company difficult because "the younger employees feel that they are owed more respect, opportunity and pay than their experience, ability or knowledge merit" (Bisceglia 2014). Hiring teams were instructed to be vigilant when interviewing millennials, to screen out ones with "the narcissistic, entitled personality traits that can make leading young workers so difficult." It's the myth of the age of entitlement in the workplace: Gen Y children were told they're special, so Gen Y workers bristle when bosses assert authority (Williams 2014). Never in history has a workforce been so fickle, so obdurate, so maddeningly self-willed.

Stereotypes of millennial workers are reinforced in scholarly articles in management journals. They portray Gen Y employees as "self-centred, entitled, narcissistic, materialistic and demanding, embodying a 'what's in it for me?' attitude in the workplace" (Papavasileiou and Lyons 2014, 2168). Business professors have called millennials "disloyal job-hoppers" with a tendency to "question authority" (ibid). They warn that "millennials 'want it all' and 'want it now,' in terms of good pay and benefits, rapid advancement, work/life balance, interesting and challenging work" (Ng, Schweitzer, and Lyons 2010, 282).

In fact, millennials have been disentitled in all kinds of ways when it comes to their role as workers. Over the past three decades, paid work arrangements have become less secure and less well compensated. Pressure from owners and investors and support from state policymakers has resulted in millennials being entitled to less of the wealth they produce on the job than workers were in the postwar decades. The so-called "gig economy" for which millennials are said to be naturally predisposed normalizes part-time, short-term, low-wage work without benefits or a pension. The gutting of publicly funded social programs intensifies challenges faced by millennial workers without paid employment. It also thrusts especially heavy burdens on millennial women, who continue to be responsible for the bulk of caretaking work in the home, despite no shortage of chatter about the collapse of traditional gender roles.

Yet as always the future remains open. Workers continue to envision a different sort of society: one centered on robust social rights and genuine democratic control in all areas of life, including the workplace. Emergent coalitions among traditional labor organizations, community groups, and new youth-led social movements are pressing for new democratic entitlements supporting our laboring lives: better wages and benefits, stronger job security, and reinvigorated social programs. Viewing the struggle over who's entitled to what and who's entitled to feel what from their perspective can deepen our thinking about what "work" is, where it happens, and in whose interests it tends to be done. It provokes us to ask whether future generations of workers ought to be entitled to more than what's available in the "new normal" of Generation Y.

DEMANDING LESS

Sedef was so nervous about applying for a summer internship with Canadian Media Incorporated (CMI)[7] that she cried several times while assembling her application. Nearing the end of her bachelor's degree in journalism, Sedef had long dreamt of landing a job in news media. She told me that she chose to major in journalism because she was "looking for something where I can raise my voice, my opinion; where I can be this independent person" (personal communication). In school she developed interviewing and writing skills, but nothing compared to the hands-on experience and networking opportunities promised by the CMI internship.

It was unfortunate that the internship would be unpaid. Sedef held $40,000 in student debt, and her family had struggled financially since

---

7 CMI is a pseudonym for an actual major Canadian media organization.

immigrating to Canada from western Asia 10 years earlier. It was not so long ago that Sedef had risen before dawn to travel an hour across the Greater Toronto Area and wait behind a furniture store in the biting cold to claim one of the handful of mattresses being given to poor families. The CMI internship pointed to new opportunities.

Being selected for the internship stands out for Sedef as one of the proudest moments of her life: "The moment I received that email, and I was invited in for an interview, and I was told there was, like, 400 applicants, and you know, there was 15 interviews, and there was just 5 people that got chosen and I was one of them ... it was just like, *I'm doing what I wanted to.* I'm standing out; I'm raising my voice; I'm independent. People want to work with me." Sedef certainly went to great lengths to work with them.

During her four months as an intern, she worked two paid jobs to make it possible to give CMI 28 hours of free work per week. On Tuesdays, Wednesdays, Thursdays, and Fridays, she boarded the bus in the suburbs around 5:20 in the morning to be at CMI's downtown offices at 7:45. She'd work until 4:00 p.m. (with a half-hour lunch break) and would often hang around after work to see if she could be of additional help, returning home by 6:30 or 7:00 p.m. On Saturdays, Sundays, and Mondays, Sedef worked from 8:00 a.m. to 3:00 p.m. at a coffee shop near her home, then down the street from 4:00 to 9:00 p.m. at a high-end retailer in the mall (which, as Sedef points out, "still only pays you minimum wage ... it doesn't matter how high-end it is!").

Sedef was assigned to a television show at CMI. Her primary job as an intern was filling gift bags for guests in the live studio audience. Sometimes the gifts—Kindles, jewelry, hair curlers—were laid out on cafeteria tables when interns arrived for their shift. Other days, Sedef's job began in the loading bay of the shipping department, carrying crates off trucks and unpacking gifts from cardboard boxes before repacking them in sparkly gift bags. Once the show began taping, frantic staff barked urgent orders at interns. After the audience left, interns cleaned up the studio, washed dishes, and waited to be given new tasks.

The constant stream of texts from managers was difficult to keep up with. Even worse was when the texts would stop. Silence might mean that the work of the intern wasn't valued. So Sedef would do things like ask senior staff if they wanted coffee, then pay with her credit card since she was totally broke. The one time that a senior staffer returned the favor, Sedef turned down the coffee offer. She didn't want to seem presumptuous. The informal system of management and compensation created intense competition among the interns, each one wanting to be seen as industrious and competent, despite their lack of training or direction.

Toward the end of the internship, Sedef decided to clean the fridge in the kitchen connected to the studio. The fridge disgusted her from the first time she saw it. Despite being used to cool food given to the studio audience, "the fridge was *mouldy!* It was a nasty place, very unhealthy, unhygienic." So one summer day, after finishing her regular cleaning tasks, Sedef filled a red bucket with hot soapy water, found an industrial-sized rubber garbage bin, got down on her hands and knees, and scrubbed the fridge. "And I *scrubbed* that fridge! And it was … it was *trash!* It was horrible." Half-eaten yogurt cups sprouting green fuzz; indiscernible goo in cardboard take-out cartons—everything gripped by whatever stickiness coated the shelves. When an expired bottle of pickles smashed on the floor, its contents soaked one of Sedef's only pair of professional pants. "You can imagine the stench."

Sedef chose to study journalism "because you're taught a lot of writing, you're taught how to research, you're taught how to present yourself, how to communicate—those things that make you a very knowledgeable, independent person." Now she was standing in a studio at one of Canada's top media corporations drenched in pickle brine, mopping up curdled milk. "And I did that, why? Because I wanted to show initiative. To feel useful, to feel like, *Hey, I can take initiative of something.* And that was the only place I could do it. In their kitchen. In their stupid store room. I hope they'll remember that, but I don't think they will. I don't even think they'll remember my name."

It's not difficult to understand why Sedef loathed the job. More complicated is the fact that she still considers herself lucky to have had it. In Sedef's view, working three jobs at once was good training for today's work world, and affiliation with big media organizations makes for distinctive lines on a CV. "I was treated like garbage," she says, but others have it even worse. The hundreds of applicants who don't get the internship, don't get the chance to get treated like garbage, are at an even greater disadvantage in a highly competitive job market. "That's what makes me feel so damn lucky."

THE NEW NORMAL AT WORK

In 2009, the president of the American Sociological Association gave a speech to fellow sociologists titled "Precarious Work, Insecure Workers: Employment Relations in Transition." Arne Kalleberg's address was a grim overview of the rise of precariousness among workers. "By 'precarious work,'" said Kalleberg, "I mean employment that is uncertain, unpredictable, and risky from the point of view of the worker" (Kalleberg 2009, 2). Precarious jobs involve "irregular or unpredictable hours and, in many instances [...] can be terminated at any time" (Hardgrove, McDowell, and Rootham 2015, 1061). A precarious worker "lacks security and stability." Sedef's story is a flesh-and-blood example of the general trends Kalleberg's research described, and it is exemplary of what one investigation describes as the recent "explosion" in unpaid internships (Hickman 2014).

The term *precarious labor* may sound obscure. But if you're a millennial worker, chances are you're intimately familiar with precarious work conditions. Short-term contracts, last-minute scheduling, unpaid internships, part-time hours (when you need full-time work), on-call shifts without compensation: These are some of the most common examples of work arrangements that depend on employee insecurity.

In the United Kingdom, one of the most widely used forms of precarious work is known as "zero-hours contracts" (Pickavance 2014). As the name suggests, workers on this contract are entitled to *zero hours* in a pay period. Employers offer hours when they need labor; people on zero-hours contracts can accept or refuse the offer. Promoters of the contract say its greater flexibility gives both managers and employees greater choice over how to use time and resources. Critics say it intensifies insecurity and anxiety in the lives of working people. Workers who fail to take all the hours offered them, no matter how few or how many, tell of being punished by not being offered additional hours in the future. They refer to this practice as being "zeroed down" or "zeroed out" by their employer. Britain's largest sporting goods retailer was estimated to have 17,000 of 20,000 workers on zero-hours contracts in 2014 (Lynam 2014).

Similar contracts, often using different names, are becoming more common throughout retail and service sectors in Canada and the United States. Judy, a millennial barista in Brooklyn, told me she'd have to wait to confirm our interview for this book because she didn't know if she was working on the weekend (personal communication). I found myself pondering how a person could care so little about their schedule—*maybe these millennials really* are *different*, I thought. Then she told me her boss never posts a schedule. He texts staff each night with instructions on who should come in for work the next day. "You don't like it?" he once asked "then work someplace else." Like virtually all baristas, Judy is not entitled to union protection. Unionized workplaces, governed by a collective agreement between employers and workers, strictly define reasonable time limits by which employees are entitled to know their work schedule. In 1984, 17 percent of (baby boomer) workers in the United States who were 30 years old were covered by a union contract. In 2014, only 5.9 percent of 30-year-old workers were unionized (Stump 2016). Precarious work is on the rise as the percentage of the workforce belonging to a union declines.

As Kalleberg (2009) noted in his presidential address, precarious work is not new to the twenty-first century. Varying degrees of insecurity on the job have existed throughout the history of paid employment. Certain sectors of the workforce—migrants, racialized people, and women, especially—have always worked disproportionately in more precarious positions. What's different in the millennial era is that precarious employment relations are becoming the new normal across all sectors of the workforce. Precariousness is "the dominant feature of the social relations between employers and workers in the contemporary world" (17). In 2016, Canada's finance minister, Bill Morneau, "told Canada's youth to get used to 'job churn'—jumping from 'job to job to job'" (Younglai 2016). The insecurity that has long been familiar to the most marginalized workers has been imposed far and wide (International Labour Organization 2015; PEPSO 2013).

Precarity is especially prevalent in the so-called "creative industries." Studies show that "unpaid interns abound in fields that are highly socially desirable, including fashion, media, and the arts" (Tokumitsu 2014). Writing copy for a fashion magazine or coding for an online start-up might be exhilarating. Certainly this kind of work forms part of a lucrative industry. But rarely does it provide jobs to individuals that come with livable, dependable wages and the likelihood of secure, long-term employment. Labor journalist Sarah Jaffe says this is partially because "the creative industry has been particularly good at convincing people that they should do the work for the love of it" (personal communication). In the ideal image of the so-called creative economy, workers move seamlessly between stimulating projects: designing websites for local firms in the morning, blogging over cappuccino in the late-day sun, making your living through your personal brand. "In reality," says Jaffe, "either you're the person who is already rich, so you can afford to do that, or you're the person who is *also* working at McDonald's, and *also* working at Starbucks, and *also* writing fifty-dollar-a-pop web pieces, hoping you're going to get paid."

Yet the creative industries are precisely where top career consultants, and many liberal arts programs, advise millennials to find work. It's no wonder, then, that wages for college graduates in the United States are "growing at historically pitiful levels." In fact, writes Derek Thompson (2014) in *The Atlantic*, "the median wage for people between the ages of 25 and 34, adjusted for inflation, has fallen in every major industry except for health care." A 2015 study by the UCLA Labor Center (2015) found that "millennials are among the lowest paid in LA County."

The creative industries, fueled by the unique experiences and skills of young people, have not been translated into a thriving class of young creative workers. In many regions—including paragons of the creative industries, such as California and the Greater Toronto Area—even a decade after the economic crash of 2008, youth unemployment still exceeds 20 per cent (Burrell and Setzer 2015; Geobey 2013). In conditions of high unemployment, low wages, and little job security, millennials are urged to pursue "alternative work arrangements" in the gig economy (Kaufman 2014).

GIG ME WITH A SPOON

Three years after graduating from Northwestern University, Sarah Kessler (2014) ran an experiment in "the gig economy." Since the 1950s, the word *gig* has been used most often in reference to the short-term work of performers, especially musicians. During the past decade, the term *gig economy* emerged as a description of the new world of "alternative employment arrangements" in which "careers will be a patchwork of temporary projects and assignments" stitched together by individuals using "apps and [online] platforms with perky names like Fancy Hands, Upwork and TaskRabbit" (Nunberg 2016). Shuttling ride seekers around as an Uber driver and renting out your apartment on Airbnb are among the best-known examples of gigs in the gig economy.

Business leaders had told Kessler (2014) and her fellow millennials that "instead of selling your soul to the Man," the gig economy empowers you

> to work for yourself on a project-by-project basis. One day it might be delivering milk, but the next it's building Ikea furniture, driving someone to the airport, hosting a stranger from out of town in your spare bedroom, or teaching a class on a topic in which you're an expert. The best part? The work will come to you, via apps on your smartphone, making the process of finding work as easy as checking your Twitter feed.

Business leaders and analysts have said that the gig economy "could be the force that saves the American worker" (Kaufman 2013). Short-term, flexible employment arrangements are portrayed as the antidote for a working-class ailing from decades of attacks on unions, wages and benefits, and social programs. Intrigued by the promise of the changing work world, Kessler threw herself into the gig economy for four weeks in 2012. Her aim was modest: make more than minimum wage through short-term jobs found online.

In her month of gigging it, Kessler was paid by different people to open mail, label photographs, dance in a flash mob, tutor a high school student, reschedule flights, and wrap presents. She unsuccessfully bid on dozens more tasks posted online. For example, her $20 bid to test a website for two hours failed; her $12 bid to pick up mail and forward it to California failed. No one accepted her offer to walk dogs, make pizza, or proofread papers. She didn't own a car, so couldn't offer rides. Her apartment was too small to rent part of it out.

In Kessler's "best-case scenario," on her most lucrative day doing gigs for eight-and-a-half hours she averaged $11 per hour. Most days she made far less money, despite spending no less time working or looking for work. And on her banner $11-per-hour day, "There was no downtime. The only break I had was a 10-minute lunch." In a feature article for the business magazine *Fast Company*, Kessler (2014) concluded that "My experiences in the gig economy raise troubling issues about what it means to be an employee today and what rights a worker, even on an assignment-by-assignment basis, is entitled to."

THE ERA OF THE GOOD WORKING-CLASS JOB

It can be hard for Gen Y to imagine, but not that long ago large and growing sections of the working class—people who work for a wage, whether computer programmers or autoworkers or elementary school teachers—could expect to hold a well-paying job with benefits, a company pension, and relatively strong job security. Inequality between rich and poor was shrinking. Currents of democratic entitlement were ascendant.

The era of the good working-class job ran from the end of World War II (in 1945) to the early 1970s (see Kalleberg 2011; Sears 1999). It was characterized by comparatively low unemployment, high rates of unionization, increasing job security, and a more equitable sharing of the wealth produced throughout society. Princeton economist and *New York Times* columnist Paul Krugman (2016) refers to this period as the "Great Compression" because it saw "a sharp reduction in income gaps."

A defining feature of the era of good working-class jobs was the expansion of legal entitlements supporting equality. This expansion was driven by labor union struggles to achieve dignity and fairness for working people. A labor union is an organization of workers that represents workers' interests on the job and across society. Throughout the 1930s and 1940s, unionized workers in textiles, auto, and other industries launched powerful strikes against employers for higher wages, more control over the labor process, safer work conditions, and the right to bargain collectively. Collective bargaining strengthens equality and fairness by preventing bosses from using divide-and-conquer strategies to drive down workplace entitlements on a worker-by-worker basis. Because collective agreements are protected by labor law, as well as the collective power of workers to pressure employers (through strikes and other workplace actions), they have traditionally provided stronger workplace entitlements to workers in unionized shops. Yet, the increasingly organized, assertive, and muscular labor movement of the mid-twentieth century won historic advances that raised the standard of living for millions of non-unionized workers, too. Union victories are responsible for child labor laws and the right to the weekend, sick leave, overtime pay, parental leave, and a host of other benefits and protections.

During these same years, the state also enshrined unprecedented new legal entitlements for all citizens. These included access to publicly funded unemployment insurance, family allowances, pensions, and more robust medical coverage. The new legal entitlements were dubbed "welfare state" programs, because they were said to serve the welfare of everyone. The flowering of the welfare state occurred partially in response to pressure from the labor movement and partially as a business-friendly strategy to avoid another economic collapse on the scale of the 1930s Great Depression.

Social scientists sometimes refer to these welfare state programs— these packages of social rights or legal entitlements—as "the social wage" (Bowles and Gintis 1982, 75). The term highlights the fact that public programs such as unemployment insurance, free schooling, and old age pensions are funded by the wealth produced by workers, which the state acquires in the form of taxes. Public services, while not appearing in the form of dollars on a paycheck, provide a higher "wage" to workers inasmuch as they satisfy people's needs without requiring a fee for service. They are social rights, not commodities; available to all on the basis of membership in a community, not restricted only to those with the money to buy them. The expansion of public services is an expansion in the power of democratic currents within the real entitlement framework. Historian Alvin Finkel (2014, 133–4) writes that by the late 1940s, there was mass "insistence upon social wage programs as worker entitlements."

The period was no workers' paradise. Workers remained under the control of their bosses, and a great deal of work was grueling and undesirable. Inequalities *among* workers played on and exacerbated existing forms of oppression. For example, many of the unions affiliated with the American Federation of Labor banned black Americans throughout the 1930s. Women were excluded from many workplaces and earned less than men for the same job. Noncitizens were prevented from accessing citizenship entitlements. Yet, in spite of the persistence of oppressive currents throughout society, the era of the good working-class job bolstered the strength of workers as a group relative to the class composed of major employers and investors. Democratic entitlements were on the rise. Decades of struggle laid the groundwork on which partial victories might have been generalized and extended.

Even a glimpse at the millennial work world shows us that this is not what transpired. Instead, starting in the 1970s, the conditions of the lowest of the low in the welfare state period became the model for all workers. Despite the fact that the sphere of democratic entitlement expanded in the postwar decades, it continued to exclude many people of color, women, people with disabilities, and poor people. The precariousness of the millennial era, therefore, isn't totally new. It's the return, intensification, and generalization of employee insecurity that had been partially ameliorated for some groups for a few decades because of working-class struggles (Post 2015). Precariousness didn't begin in the twenty-first century. It came back with a vengeance in response to a surge in working-class gains.

THE NEOLIBERAL ASSAULT

In the words of political scientist David McNally (2011, 42), from the late 1970s onward, employers and governments of all party stripes "launched a coordinated offensive to roll back union power, labor rights, and employees' wages, benefits, and conditions of work." This period of increasing rule by market forces is often referred to as the *neoliberal era*. The primacy of the market in social affairs was originally championed by classical liberals like Adam Smith in the 1800s. Hence *neo*liberalism is, literally, the new liberalism. Neoliberal social policy forces people to meet more and more needs through individual consumer transactions, not publicly funded and administered social programs. The core principle of neoliberalism is that people should not be entitled to anything other than what they can afford to buy.

Neoliberal visions began being implemented in the 1970s during the first global economic crisis since the end of World War II. At that time, the economic boom produced by postwar reconstruction fizzled. Oil prices spiked following policy changes of major oil-producing governments. Owners and employers who had long been unhappy with rising working-class entitlements saw the economic crisis as an opportunity to reset the real entitlement framework organizing the work world (Sears 2014). Corporate leaders, backed by allies in political parties, the state, and the press, proclaimed that it was impossible to run profitable businesses in a climate of elevated worker entitlements. They called for relaxing environmental regulations, making it easier for employers to hire and fire, lowering corporate taxes, boosting free trade, and scaling back the power of labor unions. It was an attack on the postwar expansion of social rights. As employers "downsized" and "restructured"—closing shops, firing staff, rolling back wages and benefits—new leadership within traditional political parties promised to strengthen the employer offensive using the tools of the state. In the Global North, Margaret Thatcher's Conservative government in Britain and Ronald Reagan's Republican administration in the United States led the charge (see Dean 2013).

Under neoliberalism, work has become more precarious for more people *because* business classes successfully undercut worker entitlements on the job and those accessible through the social wage. It is harder for millennial workers to access unemployment insurance in Canada than it was for previous generations. Recent bipartisan efforts to reform social security in the United States have been described as an exercise in "draconian benefit cuts" (Kotlikoff 2015).

Even as income inequality in the United Kingdom grows, the UK government recently cut benefits to 600,000 people with disabilities (Cowburn 2016). With the spread of anti-union laws, the percentage of the workforce covered by a union has fallen (Duke 2016). In the absence of union protections, the number of job changes expected over a worker's lifetime rose. When baby boomers were young, they could expect around 11 job changes in a working life. Millennials should expect more than 20 (Meister 2012; US Department of Labor 2016). This is the "job churn" Canada's government has told millennials to get used to. Moreover, neoliberalism exacerbates the gendered character of worker disentitlement. Not only do men continue to make more money than women for the same work, but neoliberal "employer-driven flexiblization" of scheduling adds to the challenge faced disproportionately by women of managing "the double day of household labor and wage labor" (McCrate 2012, 40). Women continue to do most of the unpaid household work (such as cleaning, shopping, and childcare), even in heterosexual couples in which both members do paid work outside the home (Miller 2015).

Economic geographer David Harvey (2007) defines changes in the real entitlement framework of the neoliberal era as being about a massive transfer of wealth and power from working people to major owners and investors. Between 2000 and 2012, while Canadian governments slashed spending on social programs, they also cut the rate at which corporations are taxed from 29 percent to 15 percent. In the United States, productivity and median wages "grew in lockstep" during the 1950s and 1960s. In other words, the wealth generated by more efficiently transforming economic inputs into outputs was shared relatively equitably among capitalists and workers. Between 1973 and 2014, the US economy grew by 72.2 percent but workers' hourly compensation rose by only 9.2 percent. Compare that to the period 1948 to 1973, when 96.7 percent economic growth was nearly matched by 91.3 percent growth in hourly compensation to workers (Economic Policy Institute 2015). Today, disproportionately high levels of new wealth produced by workers are being kept by the capitalists themselves.

Even top defenders of the existing social order can't ignore that owners are entitled to a lot more of the wealth produced in society today than they were a few decades ago. In a 2013 speech, US President Barack Obama said that by the 1980s "the link between higher productivity and people's wages was severed—the income of the top 1 percent nearly quadrupled between 1979 and 2007, while the typical family's barely budged" (in Shierholz and Mishel 2013). Wage inequality has grown strikingly during the past several decades. In 1965, corporate chief executive officers (CEOs) averaged only 20 times more than what workers made. By contrast, in 2013, the average CEO made 295 times more than the average worker (Davis and Mishel 2014). Since 1975, "nearly half of U.S. income gains went to the richest one per cent" of the population (Strachan 2014). Between 1979 and 2010, there was a drop in the proportion of US jobs offering health insurance, a retirement plan, and a real wage of $18.50 (Benanav 2015).[8] Today, income inequality is worse in the United States than any time since the 1920s (Desilver 2013).

Critics of neoliberalism hoped that the 2008 economic crisis would lead to a different way forward. However, the return to profitability— the economic "fix," at least to this point—has been the development of an even more virulent strain of neoliberalism. Governments and employers confronted the crisis with a brutal "austerity agenda." The word *austerity* refers to sternness or a severe attitude. Sociologist Alan Sears (2014, 1) defines the post-2008 "austerity agenda" as a policy project "based on slashing social programs, undercutting wages and working conditions, choking out even the limited forms of democracy that now exist and attacking migrants' rights" (see also McNally 2011, 4–5). Economist Richard Wolff (2012, 9) observes that "the mass of Americans" have been told that "everyone" needs to pay the costs of the crisis, "and that they must suffer austerity cutbacks just when they urgently need more and better government services." Five years after the end of the 2009 recession, in a period of so-called economic "recovery," the share of the population with a job (the employment–population ratio) was still lower than it had been prior to the crash. And the modest, shaky gains that were achieved by working people were unequally divided along racial and ethnic lines. White households were 13 times wealthier than black households in 2013, as

---

8 Adjusted to current prices.

compared to 7 times wealthier in 2010 (Kochhar and Fry 2014). The "new normal" of neoliberal austerity forms the grounds on which millennials must work to survive.

MILLENNIAL DISENTITLEMENT IN NEOLIBERAL TIMES

Research by Tanner Mirrlees (2015) analyzes different ways that millennial workers are portrayed in mass media. He notes that alongside assumptions about rampant narcissism in Gen Y, today's young workers are also assumed to possess unique values and skills. Yes, millennials can be feckless and entitled; but at the same time, because of their supposedly innate flexibility and expertise in all things digital, they're also often viewed as being potentially transformable into unique assets on the job. "Not only do members of Generation Y look different," writes Julie Cogin (2012, 2286), a management professor in Australia, "with their body piercings, tattoos, and electronic decorations, they behave and think differently as well." Optimistic articles in the business press interpret negative traits of the millennial worker (distractibility, expecting to be in charge) as evidence that Gen Y is specially built for the flexible labor relations that have become the new normal in the neoliberal era.

The world's largest human resources professional society declares that because millennials are "so comfortable with technology, so unaccustomed with steady incomes as the norm," they are "tailor-made for project work" (Maurer 2016). Lucky for them, writes Micha Kaufman (2014), who covers millennial issues in *Forbes*, the new normal of the gig economy is a gateway to millennial self-fulfillment: "With everyone pinging from job to job and so much being done on a project-by-project basis, new possibilities abound to reinvent your career and find ways to do what you love." Researchers at Bentley University (2014) applauded the entrepreneurial hustle of Gen Y, noting that 89 percent of millennials regularly check their work email after work hours. A *Forbes* list of "5 Things Every Boss Should Know about Working with Millennials" (Krueger 2014) included the fact that they "love (are obsessed) with entrepreneurship." Supposedly this generation is hardwired for the gig economy.

The millennial editors of the cultural criticism journal *n+1* reject this interpretation. They argue that "the image of the autonomous, free-spirited millennial" who loves entrepreneurship more than previous generations is a simplistic and inaccurate representation of a much more complex situation (n+1 2015). In their view, the idea that millennials are uniquely adaptable and entrepreneurial serves "as a way of socializing [Gen Y] into an unequal society." Millennial attitudes and aptitudes didn't cause neoliberal work arrangements; rather, millennials entered the workforce in the age of austerity and are now, quite reasonably, doing what they can to get by in it.

In the words of *n+1*, "This is why millennials are constantly figured as happily zigzagging from job to job, fleeing long-term employment, luxuriating in the intense anxiety of a precariousness said to be uniquely theirs." If they're not doing that, something's wrong with them (hint: they're insufferably entitled). The new world of work requires new generations of workers to "take charge of our own lives," sell themselves, build their personal brand, diversify their skills. Miya Tokumitsu (2014) writes that "there's little doubt that 'do what you love' (DWYL) is now the unofficial work mantra for our time." The mantra might sound nice, but for most wage workers in the neoliberal economy it's not a genuine option. Even worse, argues Tokumitsu, within the DWYL paradigm, "unlovable but socially necessary work," like emptying office wastebaskets or working nightshifts at the hospital, becomes devalued or ignored.

Gen Y wants it this way, though, right? Trend followers tell us millennials are "fickle," easily bored when the scenery isn't changing (Court 2016). Yet economist Gerald Friedman says that "Given a choice, workers choose careers and jobs, not freelance gigs" (in Parramore 2014). A 23-year-old editor of a Toronto-based start-up online lifestyle magazine told me she understands why she's working more than 60 hours a week for less than 30 hours pay. "We're new, and we're still building our brand. I mean, I love the work—the excitement, the challenge of doing new things all the time. We just don't have a business model that can pay everyone what they're worth right now" (personal communication). What does she dream of five years into the future? Not new ventures, not greater risks, not a change of scenery: "You know—a salary, I guess? Some reassurance that it's not just all going to fall apart the next day." Fair compensation and job security: these seem like reasonable hopes. But in the new normal of neoliberal work relations, to expect such things is to reinforce the myth that millennial workers are plagued by the entitlement epidemic.

Sociologists Shaun Wilson and Norbert Ebert (2013, 264) write that millennials have come of age in "the precarious work society." In their words, "job precarity translates into social precarity" (270). People living in precarious-work societies have a harder time securing the basics of life, especially stable, adequate housing. When uncertainty is part of business-as-usual, "norms of self-exploitation" become widespread (264). This can lead people struggling with heightened anxieties into "negative forms of coping," such as substance abuse (266). Precariousness can stoke hostility toward immigrants when un- and underemployed citizens look to blame someone for their hardship.

Sociologist Richard Sennett (1999) shows that fragmented work arrangements make it more difficult to form robust social and political attachments. They also inhibit people's ability to develop coherent senses of themselves as productive workers and community members. Cultural theorist Lauren Berlant (2011) argues that fragmentation within the precarious-work society has led to a collective lowering of expectations among workers. In contrast to the more expansive dreams of economic security available to more people in the era of the good working-class job, today it can seem more reasonable to dream of a "less-bad bad life" (137–8). Recall that in the absence of an alternative path into her profession, Sedef felt lucky to land an unpaid internship in which she was "treated like garbage."

THE PAST IS PRESENT

In 2016, *Forbes* published a cartoon captioned "'The Gig Economy,' the Early Years." In the sepia tones associated with old-time photographs, the cartoon's single image depicts a large group of men standing next to large steam ships. Dozens of men in plaid shirts, suspenders, caps, and other symbols of the working class crowd around a lone man in a suit. The be-suited man is pointing his finger and appears to be barking orders. A short paragraph beneath the cartoon explains what's going on:

> In the 19th century and during the first half of the 20th, many American workers submitted to the "shape up," a daily ritual of outbidding one another for the chance of work, as seen in the classic film *On the Waterfront*, starring Marlon Brando. Now we have Airbnb, Uber and other "gig economy" jobs that "liberate" employees from the drudgery of the 9-to-5. (Anderson 2016)

The *Forbes* cartoon reminds us that in addition to what's unique about precariousness in the so-called new economy, exploitation at the workplace and insecurity among all layers of the workforce are not unique to the millennial era. The newness of millennial disentitlement in the precarious-work society is part of historical struggles that have normalized particular forms of oppression at work over generations.

What's true about wage labor in the twenty-first century has been true since wage labor became the dominant work arrangement in the 1800s: wage laborers don't get to choose what they'll produce, nor do they control the fruits of their labor. Employers are entitled to the time of the wage laborer, and employers control decisions over the labor process. The real entitlement framework organizing the contemporary economy is structured by centuries-old inequalities lying at the core of capitalism.

Assuming that millennial workers are freely in control of their life-course makes it easier to accuse them of being undeservedly demanding when they bristle at the confines and deprivations of their workplaces, ask for raises, shirk responsibilities, or dream of running the show. It's more difficult to cast young people as being uniquely spoiled if it's acknowledged that they, like everyone else who doesn't live off wealth produced by others, are compelled to spend most of their time laboring in exchange for wages. Capitalists live off the profits generated through the labor of most of the population who don't own means for reproducing subsistence. Owners and investors don't plant the seeds, fly the planes, build the computers, or do anything else to make the goods and services that are the source of capitalist profits. Those things are done by millions of waged truck drivers, office clerks, cashiers, farm laborers, computer coders, and other workers.

If you don't own a profitable office or factory or industrial farm, you really have no choice but to sell your ability to work. If you want to eat, sleep under a roof, and enjoy even a modicum of comfort in other areas of your life, you need the wage an employer will trade you for your laboring power. The very system of private property and wage labor effectively entitles employers and investors to the labor of a class of workers who have no survival options other than selling their power to labor for a wage. That's a buyer's market, if there ever was one.

Yet employer entitlements don't end with "the silent compulsion of economic relations" that presses workers to seek wage-labor arrangements to support purchasing the goods and services they want and need (Marx [1867] 1976, 889). The actual exchange of hours worked for wages, despite appearing to be an equal trade on the surface, in fact generates further inequality between employers and employees. To grow, to be profitable, owners claim full control over the value that workers create in excess of the employer's starting costs. Owners call it profit. Critical political economists call it "surplus value," because it's generated by products and services that workers produce but aren't paid for (Wolff 2012, 2). It's debatable whether you think this sort of exploitation is necessary; what's certain is that a deeply unequal set of entitlement relationships lies at the heart of the wage-labor system of work.

Profit making also depends on vast amounts of unpaid labor that people do outside the workplace, primarily in private homes (Ferguson and McNally 2015; Vogel [1983] 2014). In order for workers to labor on the job and create profits for employers, there are endless meals to be cooked, groceries to buy, teeth to be brushed, clothes to be washed, and floors to be swept and mopped. Industry needs a workforce not only tomorrow but into the distant future. This involves additional layers of reproductive work: raising children, tending to the sick, settling migrants, and ensuring healthy pregnancies. Yet most of this work is done at virtually no cost to employers. Work within a capitalist economy strictly separates workers' profit-producing laboring time (which employers want) from the time necessary for workers to eat, heal, become educated, love, and play. Employers want nothing to do with this unprofitable time.

The unequal gender dynamics prevailing under capitalism mean that women have been responsible for doing the bulk of this unpaid reproductive work. A recent study by two Ohio State sociologists shows that after a heterosexual couple has a child, the woman's work increases by 21 hours per week, while the man's increases by only 12.5 hours (Miller 2015). As the first austerity cuts were being implemented in the wake of the 2008 recession, political theorist Silvia Federici observed that "it is clearly expected that in the aftermath of the new cuts women will make up for the loss" (in Naylor 2012). It's no stretch to say, then, that business classes are entitled to the economic benefits of a sexist division of labor, and that gender inequality is reinforced through profit-making-as-usual. Millennial workers are being disentitled by the austerity agenda; but workers have always been disentitled under capitalism, and capitalist exploitation has always depended on gender oppression.

Yet oppressive entitlements shaping laboring lives, even while spreading and calcifying, have never been fully secured. They have always been contested by workers, peasants, and others whose lives are degraded by them. This is no less true in the millennial era. Coordinated pressure for the expansion of worker entitlements has weakened under neoliberalism, but new experiments are always developing, even if unevenly and outside the mainstream news cycle. Sometimes they burst onto the public stage, capturing media attention and reinvigorating workers' imaginations.

EXPANDING WORKER ENTITLEMENTS IN THE MILLENNIAL ERA

On 17 September 2011, activists in New York City took over a small park in Lower Manhattan, the symbolic center of global capitalism. The occupation of Zuccotti Park quickly grew into one of the largest and most inspiring movements for the expansion of democratic entitlements of the millennial era (see Graeber 2013; van Gelder 2011). The Gen Y activists at the center of the movement rallied around the slogan "Occupy Wall Street." They combined anger at bankers and corporate leaders who benefit from precarious work arrangements with hope for greater economic equality and participatory democracy. Within a month, Occupy protests were happening in more than 180 cities globally.

In terms that soon became part of everyday conversations, Occupiers condemned the massive wealth and power accumulated by "the 1 percent"—the top income earners, heads of major corporations, major bankers, and their state supporters—and called on "the 99 percent"—the rest of the population—to demand its fair share of the world's wealth and power. A Tumblr called "We Are The 99 Percent" invited people to post selfies while holding a short written statement describing their personal struggles. The following three examples, posted in October 2011, evoke several key themes of the movement:

> I'm a 31 y/o female with a bachelor's of science in kinesiology. I haven't been able to find a job in my field so I'm currently working my BUTT OFF managing a bakery for less than $20,000/year. I'm in collections on EVERYTHING and I live in constant fear that the next asthma attack I have will be the one that takes my life. I am the 99%. (We Are The 99 Percent 2011a)

****

> I am 24. I have over $100K in student loan debt. Wells Fargo expects me to pay at least $800/month and garnished $400 from my bank account. I'm now looking for two part-time jobs to get by and afraid I won't be able to pay rent or even eat well. I just wanted to take pictures. My parents are going to lose their house. Forgive student loan debt. We are the 99%. (We Are The 99 Percent 2011b)

****

> I have a master of arts degree in women's studies. However, the only job I can find is as a bartender at a local restaurant. I owe over 60K in student loans. I am forced to rely on food stamps and W.I.C. to support my son. Is this the "American Dream" I worked so hard for? I am the 99%. (We Are The 99 Percent 2011c)

Stronger worker entitlements formed part of the core of the Occupy vision—better wages, job security, pensions, and workplace benefits for all. Representatives of traditional labor unions stood alongside crowds of nonunionized paid and unpaid workers. In a particularly striking image of working-class solidarity, hundreds of members of the Air Line Pilots Association, many of them dressed in their official pilots' uniforms, joined Occupy activists on Wall Street during a rally in late September.

For a few months that autumn, Occupy provided concrete spaces and a common language with which to strengthen shared senses of democratic entitlement. By early 2012, nearly all Occupy encampments were gone. Many were destroyed during violent attacks by police. Although Occupy's ultimate goal of ending the rule of the 1 percent was not successful, the movement contributed to the political development of a whole new generation of activists and workers. Occupy placed inequality and radical democracy at the center of public debate in ways that hadn't been the case before 2011. It was the first mass movement in North America for economic, social, and environmental justice that the millennial generation not only participated in but played key roles in organizing. It put a sudden and dramatic point on the fact that struggles over who is entitled to organize and control the production of goods and services remain very much open. The movement provided a living sense that an alternative political vision is possible.

Only months after the destruction of the last Occupy encampment, New York City was again home to a new wave of worker mobilization. Before dawn on 29 November 2012, a group of McDonald's employees gathered in the cold in front of their store in Midtown Manhattan. Of the 17 employees scheduled for the morning shift, 14 refused to work. These workers put their jobs at risk, and gave up a day's pay, to disrupt McBusiness-as-usual in a demonstration for fairer wages and the right to union protections. By sun up, similar strikes had been launched at dozens of Burger King, Kentucky Fried Chicken, Taco Bell, and Wendy's restaurants.

At the Midtown McDonald's, striking workers rallied on the sidewalk alongside community supporters and coworkers with the day off. Wearing a black hooded coat and a black baseball cap, 21-year-old

McDonald's worker Raymond Lopez yelled to the crowd, "When the people on the bottom move, the people on the top fall! The reason they're on the top is that we're holding them up!" (in *Democracy Now* 2012). Before the end of the day, 200 fast-food workers walked off the job in New York. The *New York Times* described it as "the biggest wave of job actions in the history of America's fast-food industry" (Greenhouse 2012). It kicked off a movement that soon surged across the country, winning not only widespread public support for low-income workers but significant pay increases in numerous jurisdictions.

Fast-food workers make up one of the largest sections of the US labor force, and more than 60 percent of fast-food workers are members of Generation Y. Yet virtually none of the workers in the 200,000 fast-food restaurants in the United States are unionized. In the absence of union protections, workers can be easily disciplined and fired. This is one of the reasons why wages in the industry, which are largely *millennial* wages, remain so low. At the time of the 2012 strikes, more than two-thirds of fast-food workers made between $7.26 and $10.09 an hour. Even if they could get full-time work, a rarity in the precarious-work society, their yearly wage would still be as little as $13,200 (Pylayev 2013).

In 2013, one-day strikes were held in New York, Chicago, Seattle, Los Angeles, and three other cities. Actions combined local grassroots organizing with financial and organizational support from the Service Employees International Union, the second-largest national union in the country. Labor journalists Josh Eidelson and Sarah Jaffe (2013) declared that what had been a series of local protests was now a national movement.

At first, restaurant owners and management dismissed worker demands by telling employees to lower their expectations. Burger King announced that it offers employees "compensation and benefits that are consistent with the quick-service restaurant industry" (in Frumkin 2012). In other words, management is justified in paying workers poverty wages because that's what all the corporations do. Management at McDonald's published an online guide instructing workers how to make do with the little they have. "Workers were advised to break food into pieces to make it go farther, sing to relieve stress, and take at least two vacations a year" (Finnegan 2014). The main organization representing fast-food franchise owners called the protests a "public relations campaign designed to mislead the public and policymakers" (Greenhouse and Kasperkevic 2015). Some employers fired workers involved in the Fight for $15. Yet in the face of this counterattack, the movement continued to grow.

On 15 April 2015, more than 60,000 fast-food workers participated in one-day strikes and demonstrations in nearly 240 cities in the United States and another 100 cities globally. Students on 170 US college campuses participated in the day of action. Labor unions representing nurses, airport workers, teachers, and truckers marched in solidarity. In Milwaukee, Wisconsin, 19-year-old McDonald's worker Tashayla Harper attended her first protest. She was inspired to join the Fight for $15 by her one-year-old daughter. Holding the girl in her arms, Tashayla said, "I work, and I only make $7.25, and that little money goes on my daughter. I never have enough for myself. [...] It's at the point where I can't even afford my own house, because I don't make enough. I rely on those food stamps every month" (in Kasperkevic 2015). Three months after the April demonstrations, fast-food workers won their biggest victory to date. Governor Andrew Cuomo announced that New York State would raise minimum wage for fast-food workers to $15 by 2018 (Cuomo 2016).[9]

The Fight for $15 is not a blueprint for millennial workers; no single campaign is. It is, however, a case study demonstrating the co-development of working-class material and emotional entitlements. Fast-food workers have shown how struggles for immediate, winnable legal entitlements (i.e., higher wages) can fuel shared senses of entitlement to broadening social rights and collective worker power, even among workers who have long felt isolated and doubtful about workplace improvements. Winning modest reforms through the self-organization of mass coalitions strengthens the grounds on which to press for additional demands that would further transform the world of work toward equality and democracy. Millennial campaigns

---

9 The pledge was signed into law on 4 April 2016 as part of the 2016–17 state budget.

with the collective power to expand social rights and democracy will require new experiments in drawing together even larger and more robust community–labor coalitions. The most successful experiments will involve not only workers of all ages across industries, but waged and unwaged workers, unionized and nonunionized workers, migrant workers, low-income workers, as well as more privileged layers of the working class.

GETTING A LIFE

This chapter has challenged the assumption that the narrative of the overly entitled millennial worker developed because millennials are hardwired differently than workers in previous generations. Certainly there are high-flying young people making a fortune on the stock market and leading profitable companies. Yes, there are millennials making six figures a year riding the Google Bus through San Francisco's gentrified streets to the tech behemoth's mothership in Mountain View, California. But economic success is not the defining story of the millennial generation.

Economic security is the story of a particular fraction of people in their late teens to late thirties, a fraction that has more in common with privileged classes in previous generations than with the less-privileged majority of millennials. The age of entitlement myth depicts the advantages of a select group of comparatively well-off young people as though their situation was the experience of Gen Y as a whole. This undercuts the authority of all claims to deserve more, including those operating in the service of democracy and equality.

In the millennial era, owners and investors have forced workers to accept more flexible work arrangements. The severe weakening of organized resistance to neoliberal work arrangements has allowed precariousness across all sectors of the working class to be normalized. Today, any expectations among workers that exceed the new normal are more easily labeled "entitled." Paradoxically, then, it's in the context of rising currents of employer-friendly oppressive entitlement that the myth of millennial entitlement has emerged. The myth reflects and provides ideological support for an economic perspective primarily concerned about enhancing business profitability at the expense of working people's standards of living.

The age of entitlement myth helps to legitimize the austerity agenda that tells workers to expect less on the job and through the social wage. It aims to justify the extension of the rule of the market and equates citizenship with individual consumer activity. If the oppressive consequences of neoliberalism are going to be halted, and the twenty-first century is to become a new era of democracy and equality, millennial workers will have to reject the myth by organizing on the job, and in their homes and communities, for stronger worker compensation, protection, benefits, and collective decision-making power.

Kathi Weeks (2011, 231–3) argues that stronger work entitlements aren't just about getting a good job; they're about "getting a life." The real value of things like adequate pay, health care and a pension, vacation time, and some degree of control over the labor process is that they help people live fuller, healthier, more meaningful lives— not just on the job, but outside of formal work arrangements. When people talk about "work" today, they're almost always referring to wage labor, and that's been the focus of this chapter. As if the stakes of who's entitled to what regarding *on-the-job* work weren't already important enough, they get even higher when we conceive of work in the broadest sense of the human capacity to transform the world through our thoughts and actions.

Imagining a different future and acting to make it into reality is daunting. It certainly seemed impossible to many people during the Great Depression of the 1930s, as banks collapsed, the unemployment rate soared to 25 percent, and hundreds of thousands of people were evicted from their homes. Yet within decades working people had changed the world momentously. In winning gains at work and huge increases in the social wage through the postwar welfare state, mass grassroots mobilizations and working-class organizations proved that making a fairer, more equitable future is both conceivable and possible. All of us already do transformative work all the time: paid work, artistic work, domestic work, emotional work. The issue is who coordinates it and toward what ends we work. Absolutely the challenges before us are daunting; but not for the first time in the history of working-class struggles has the terrain of battle been inauspicious. And just as the future was open to the forces of resistance in the dire days of the Great Depression, the future is open today. Your actions will play a part in making the history of tomorrow. Where are the efforts to strengthen worker entitlements within your sphere of influence? How might you contribute to them?

Postsecondary campuses are key sites of coordinating ideas and action in the millennial era. They are sites of struggle between those seeking to destroy the remaining vestiges of working-class entitlement and social movements that are reimagining a new world of democratic entitlement. Struggle on campus is the focus of Chapter 4.

CHAPTER FOUR

AUSTERITY U: TEACHING AND RESISTING DISENTITLEMENT ON CAMPUS

GETTING SCHOOLED

The millennial generation is the most educated cohort in history. In 1940 in the United States, only 5 percent of the population over 25 years of age held a bachelor's degree or higher (Ryan and Bauman 2016). By 2015, this percentage stood at 33 percent. Another 18 percent had completed some postsecondary schooling (US Department of Education 2015). The higher education participation rate in the United Kingdom has hovered around 50 percent since 2011 (Times Higher Education 2013). In Canada, during the first decade of the new millennium, student enrollment in higher education grew by "a whopping 44 per cent" (Charbonneau 2011). College education is a defining feature of the millennial condition and is part of the millennial passport to success.

That's not to say that every member of Gen Y goes to college or university. Roughly half of millennials won't end up with a degree. But college is no less relevant in shaping the identity of millennials who don't go to college than those who do. The lifetime earnings of degree-holders are said to be more than $1 million more than non-degree-holders (Fottrell 2015). It's not easy to come up with examples of millennials on popular TV shows or films that aren't college grads, in college, or expecting to attend college in the future. Don't go to school? Get left out of the picture. The consequences of educational disparity are more severe in the millennial era.

Yet even as college has become part of the millennial norm, millennial students are ambivalent about what they get out of higher education. A first-year student in a class I teach who hopes to work in community health told me "I don't expect the degree will get me hired anywhere. But I'm pretty sure I'm screwed without it." Even as millennials make up the most educated generation in history, they're also facing increasing precariousness in the labor market and cuts to the social safety net, as discussed in Chapter 3.

Students like learning about the world and meeting new friends. At the same time, they often feel stressed and isolated by academic routines and social hierarchies on campus. Many move from one large lecture hall to the next feeling like insignificant numbers, not like important human beings with unique ideas, problems, and questions. University brochures, frat-boy movies, and nostalgic elders make it seem as though the college years are the best of your life. But the millennial student population is one in which one in five women will be sexually assaulted (Anderson and Clement 2015), and racism continues to structure life on many campuses. The average millennial graduate holds tens of thousands of dollars in student debt. No wonder students are frequently overheard asking each other "What am I really getting out of this?"

Political and business elites aren't happy with the state of post-secondary education (PSE) either. Most support the expansion of higher education in principle, but business leaders, politicians, and pundits complain that schools aren't preparing young people for the real world of the changing economy. There's constant chatter about a "skills shortage" because our schools aren't teaching kids right. Publicly subsidized colleges and universities are framed as relics of the welfare state; their costs are blamed for high taxes.

Efforts to reform or demolish higher education are in high gear all around the world. There are contending visions of what PSE for the twenty-first century should look like. Each is rooted in much broader assumptions about who is entitled to access what resources and who is entitled to feel what. Reform efforts focus primarily on schooling, but each also reflects a different vision of how society ought to work.

The leading edge of PSE reform aims to retool the millennial postsecondary system to better serve the needs of the neoliberal society. The core aim of the emergent neoliberal university, what I call Austerity U, is to prepare millennial citizen-consumers and workers for the precarious work society discussed in Chapter 3.[10] Policies pushing PSE in this direction are part of the broader project of extending the rule of the market and disentitling citizens and workers from having their needs met except through what they can afford to buy. Austerity U is about teaching disentitlement.

In the face of Austerity U's rapid advance, student movements are resisting efforts to disentitle them of the education they deserve. These movements frame postsecondary education as a pillar of democracy, which should therefore be accessible to all. Arguing that education is a social right, student campaigns focus on the problem of rising tuition and student debt and have attacked discrimination of all kinds. The largest and most successful movements are fighting battles not only to defend the best of the PSE system that emerged during the broad welfare state period, but also for alternative transformations rooted in commitments to democratic entitlement.

The question is not whether changes are coming to millennial campuses and the schools of Generation Z. Changes are happening fast; many more are soon to come. The question is whether transformation will be driven by the currents of oppressive entitlement feeding Austerity U, or whether student-led movements for democratic entitlement can lay the basis for a postsecondary system oriented toward achieving genuine equity and the satisfaction of human needs. Campuses are key sites of struggle shaping society's real entitlement framework.

THE QUEBEC SPRING

On 22 May 2012 I was one of several hundred thousand people wearing a small red square pinned to their jacket while marching

---

10 Thanks to Alan Sears for coining this term in an article we co-wrote a few years ago (see Sears and Cairns 2014).

jubilantly through the sunny spring streets of Montreal, Quebec. The red square, or *carré rouge*, was the core symbol of the 2012 Quebec student strike. The symbol took shape out of the French saying "*carrément dans le rouge*," which refers to being "squarely in the red" (Messer 2012). To be squarely in the red means to be deep in debt, a position more and more millennial students know well. Adopting the red square as a symbol of student struggle was a way of highlighting the shared experience of financial hardship that's become the norm for thousands of Gen Y students.

In March 2011 the government of Quebec announced plans to raise tuition by 75 percent. Only hours after the announcement, Université du Québec à Montréal student organizer Alfonse Seguin joined several hundred students in a protest. He thought to himself, "OK, we are able to mobilize; this is quite good" (personal communication). Student unions and campus groups campaigned for a tuition freeze throughout the fall of 2011. They wrote letters to elected representatives. They published open letters calling on the government to change its plans. The government flatly rejected these pleas in the name of financial necessity. The tuition hike was a central plank of the government's austerity budget. The premier declared that the hike was non-negotiable: The policy would be implemented.

Students escalated their resistance. They occupied university buildings, blocked traffic, and held sit-ins at government offices. On 10 November, all the main student unions launched a one-day strike. In Seguin's view, "it was a tremendous success. We had 200,000 people on strike; 30,000 people in the street. It was the largest rally, outside of a general strike, in the history of Quebec. It was just crazy. Yeah. It was like … that day I cried. I cried when I saw all the people in the street. I was just like … oh my God!" In mass student assemblies throughout the fall, students debated and approved mandates for a general, continuous strike.

Assembly democracy is a highly participatory form of rule by the people designed to ensure that all members of a community are able to play an active role in decision making. These particular assemblies operated at the campus or program level. Membership in the decision-making bodies of the large student unions ran into the tens of thousands. Seguin's department formed an assembly of around 700 students. He knows this because that's the capacity of the room they met in, and the room was filled to capacity. In his words, participating in student assemblies "creates a sense of empowerment. You know, speaking in front of 700 people, and seeing people listening, nodding, going like this [making twinkly fingers, he explained that student assemblies adhere to a no-clapping policy, to ensure everyone can hear voices at the front of the room]. You see all these people, and there's this sense that we're making decisions together."

A small minority of students argued against a strike. They too opposed the tuition hike, but they feared disrupting the school year would jeopardize their graduation plans. Seguin recalls that the response to this minority included a sense of generational responsibility. Taking the floor in student assemblies, "we would mobilize arguments based on the need for solidarity" among students today and with generations past and future:

> Yes, we will all make sacrifices by going on strike. Everybody will need to postpone their career in some way, but it won't be for that long. [...] And we need to be able to make some kind of sacrifice because of our link to the history of the Quebec student movement. The fact that we can all go to school today, and the fact that our tuition fees are lower than in any other province, is because there have been six other strikes before now. Generation after generation made the sacrifice to go on strike for lower tuition. Today it's our turn to make the sacrifice and defend higher education for later generations.

Before the end of 2011, dozens of assemblies representing thousands of students voted overwhelmingly in favor of striking if the government refused to cancel the tuition hike. Not all students participated in the assemblies. But, Seguin says, virtually all respected the decision to strike "because they recognized that the vote was legitimate and democratic."

By the end of May 2012, more than 200,000 Quebec students were on an "unlimited general strike" (Savard and Charaoui 2012). The strike's aim was not simply to demonstrate frustration, but to completely shut down "all courses on campus: no classes, no exams and no evaluations." The strategic logic behind the action assumed that a sufficiently large and sustained strike could force officials to make policy concessions: "Universities and colleges affected by the strike see their academic calendars disrupted, and since no classes or grading is allowed to happen, degrees can't be awarded."

The Quebec government tried to crush the strike with force. It passed an emergency law, Bill 78, which terminated the school year, made it illegal to gather in groups of 50 or more without approval by police, and threatened strike leaders with massive fines and arrest. Yet on 22 May, even after Bill 78 was law, students led the largest demonstration in the history of Quebec and Canada.

To say that the 22 May march was festive doesn't even begin to capture the energy in the streets. There were drummers and horns; whole bands passed by. Creative variations on the red square were everywhere. There were cardboard boxes wrapped in red paper transformed into helmets with eyeholes. Huge humanoid red squares looked over the crowd with defiant glares painted on protestors' placards. A woman on the sixth floor balcony of a retirement home cheered on marchers while holding up a square red couch cushion. People waved flags. My sister hugged an 8-foot-tall purple Teletubbie who appeared in the street to cheer on the students. Everywhere handmade signs bobbed overhead. On one sign the words "Loi 78" (Law 78) broke the stem on the scales of justice. Another depicted dozens of tiny red squares in the soil surrounding the roots of a flourishing tree. Above the tree were the words "BIENVENUE AU PRINTEMPS QUEBECOIS" (Welcome to the Quebec Spring). The sign around a dog's neck asked, "Ou est la democratie?" (Where is democracy?)

The Canadian Broadcasting Corporation guessed that 400,000 people marched. Others put the size of the crowd closer to half a million. Participants in the demonstration included representatives from labor unions, community organizations, and concerned citizens not affiliated with any group. City of Montreal workers cheered the demonstrators, some wearing the red square on their fluorescent safety vests. Hands with thumbs up reached out of passing cars. People waved from inside restaurants.

The student movement's success at drawing links between issues on and off campus is reflective of the fact that the symbol of the red square had a second meaning, too. It evoked the radical democratic vision and collective power of what had come to be known in 2011 as "the movements of the squares." Many of the largest and most powerful democratic movements that emerged in the wake of the economic crisis—from Tahrir Square in Cairo to the *indignados* (indigent) of Madrid to Occupy Wall Street in New York—were rooted in a public square. Students in Quebec urged people to recognize the importance of developing "shared, participatory democracy" in our schools, neighborhoods, and workplaces, "whether we are students or not" (CLASSE 2012). They framed their strike as part of broader global movements for social justice. The fight for student entitlements was a fight for democratic entitlements everywhere.

The provincial government didn't instruct police to break up the 22 May rally. It didn't have much of a choice. When mass demonstrations reach a certain size and durability, protestors assume a degree of control over the situation not available to them when their efforts are fragmented and episodic. The government could no longer pretend that it was business as usual. Students had forced the end of the term and enjoyed broad public support.

On 1 August the government resigned. By calling an election, it cleared the legislative slate, effectively cancelling the tuition hike. The students claimed victory for a vision of postsecondary education as a public good—a social right to which everyone is entitled. The movement manifesto issued by the largest student union in the province declared that "education cannot be sold; it ought to be provided to each and every one of us, without regard to our immigration status or our condition. Our aim is for an educational system that is for us, that we will share together" (ibid.)

TEACHING A WORLDVIEW

Schooling teaches a great deal more than answers for the final exam. Sociologist Alan Sears (2003, 7) writes that "students learn a world view through the educational system." Whether students major in trigonometry, the Trojan Wars, or management, common elements of the official schooling experience reinforce particular ways of understanding the line between legitimate and illegitimate behavior, ideas, and expectations. There are messages about what's acceptable and what's out of bounds in the way the classroom is organized, how universities are paid for, institutional governance models, and norms of discussion and debate. Schools not only instruct students in academic knowledge, but in how to think about themselves as future employees and citizens of the nation.

Struggles over the form and purpose of postsecondary schooling are therefore struggles over different visions of society. Student leaders of the strike in Quebec talked about education as "a training ground for humanity" (CLASSE 2012). "Our educational system," they wrote, has the potential "to allow us to pave the way towards freeing society as a whole; it can provide a liberating education that will lay the foundation for self-determination." At this moment, their vision of postsecondary education as a social right that helps deepen and extend democratic control throughout society remains a dream. But, they argue, it's a dream worth struggling for on the grounds of partial victories to date.

Quebec is not the only place where mass student power has defended and extended democratic entitlements on campus in recent years. In Chile, mass student protests erupted in 2011 after the government threatened to raise tuition and impose new user fees. In fall 2015, a national student movement in South Africa forced the government to cancel plans to hike tuition by 10 percent. Black students led the movement, highlighting the severe damage that high tuition inflicts on poorer black communities.

However, at this point in the millennial era, few places are home to activist infrastructures as durable and extensive as Quebec, Chile, and South Africa. And in the absence of sustainable political organizations, it is difficult to translate the frustrations and hopes that can be found among millennial students everywhere into effective forces of change. Yet as Quebec and a handful of other examples show, in some places at some times the organizational capacities exist to transform anger into a viable fighting force for a truly democratic alternative vision of schooling.

Notwithstanding their size and audacity of vision, the largest and best organized Gen Y student movements have largely waged defensive campaigns against the much more aggressive push for PSE reform in the neoliberal tradition. The consequences of neoliberal schooling reform are not restricted to adjustments on campus. Neoliberal schooling is also "a training ground for humanity," one that tilts the real entitlement framework throughout society in ways that favor business and political elites (CLASSE 2012).

As discussed in Chapter 3, neoliberal society is about replacing the more socialized, regulated socioeconomic model of the welfare state period with institutions governed exclusively by market mechanisms and individual consumer choice. Neoliberal society depends on extreme "employee flexibility" in the labor market, restricting union power, and the eradication of nonmarket survival alternatives, such as unemployment insurance, welfare, and publicly funded postsecondary education (McCrate 2012). Aspects of the PSE system that developed during the welfare state period obstruct the smooth transition to a fully neoliberal society. Advocates of neoliberal PSE reform also recognize that schooling teaches a worldview. The worldview they support is at odds with the one that shaped the rise of the mass university in the middle of the twentieth century.

THE RISE OF THE MASS UNIVERSITY

The decades surrounding World War II were rocked by social disruption. The Great Depression of the 1930s impoverished millions. Between 1939 and 1945, war imposed devastating material and emotional sacrifices. After the war, citizen-soldiers and their families demanded stronger support from the state to which they'd given so much. Mass militant working-class strikes fought for greater economic security and the right to collective bargaining. Campaigns against racial segregation disrupted businesses, schools, and electoral politics throughout the 1950s and 1960s. Previously excluded groups were fighting for the protections and benefits of full citizenship.

One way that Western governments tried to counter social fragmentation was by investing heavily in a massive expansion of postsecondary education. Prior to the 1940s, postsecondary education was virtually closed to all but those at the top of the social hierarchy. Economists Bowles and Gintis (1976) show that college enrollment expanded somewhat in the first half of the twentieth century to meet industry's need for a new army of office workers, technicians, and other semi-skilled bureaucrats. The development of "the corporate economy" between the 1890s and 1930s created thousands of management and administrative occupations within emergent mass corporations like Ford and General Electric (180–200). Children of the wealthy and powerful continued to receive training for lives of rule at exclusive top-tier schools (like Harvard, Princeton, and Columbia). But new and expanding middle- and lower-tier schools now offered new programs in management, accounting, urban planning, and other technical and professional arts, training a growing cohort of workers for lives in new occupational strata.

After World War II, by making college more accessible to the masses, governments sought to help "produce the world's most advanced labor force" and strengthen national ties among citizens (Harris 2015). In the United States, the GI Bill of 1944 offered free college education to all returning servicemen. Building new state schools with low or no tuition and administering generous systems of government grants made it possible for middle-income families to send their children to college. Pressed by civil rights movements, the federal government intervened to desegregate college campuses in the 1960s.

The rise of the mass university was among the welfare state's main "inclusion strategies," inviting citizens to look to the state for meeting key needs of modern life (Sears 2003, 11). It vastly expanded the proportion of the population able to access a core institution of citizenship formation, and it raised people's expectations about the value of citizenship. New layers of the population laid claim to the official knowledge and culture transferred through higher education. They also laid claim to improved chances at landing a well-paying, secure career after graduation. In exchange, students were expected to develop the discipline required of workers within a corporate hierarchy and the loyalty needed of citizens within the nation.

As more and more women, people of color, and working-class people fought their way into college, campuses became more vibrant political and social spaces. Schools were pressed to change traditional curriculum and integrate the histories of marginalized populations that hadn't previously been recognized as subjects worthy of study. In the late 1960s, especially, militant student movements demanded the creation of programs in black studies, women's studies, Indigenous studies, and labor history. Through demonstrations, strikes, and occupations, students won the right for at least minimal representation on university governing bodies.

An expanded postsecondary system still served industry's needs for a mass disciplined workforce, as well as for bases of military and technological development. Severe discrimination continued on campus. Poor and undocumented people continued to be excluded altogether. However, currents of democratic entitlement shaping the rise of the mass university expanded both the legal entitlements of citizens and the proportion of the population claiming full citizenship. The PSE system was drastically changed through struggles from below for universal access to core institutions of the nation and struggles from above to subsume social conflict within the official institutions of the state.

To the extent that the welfare state model of the mass university cultivates student expectations of being entitled to at least some basic standard of living outside the market, the postwar model of the mass university is an obstacle to the development of neoliberalism. The contradictions between what the current PSE system does and the kind of worker-citizen the neoliberal economy needs drive the most prominent PSE reform efforts in the millennial era. Generally speaking, the aim of this reform movement is to transform mass education into a training ground for life without a safety net in a precarious economy. The neoliberal model of society and the economy needs Austerity U.

MAKING AUSTERITY U

Austerity U aims to prepare the next generation of citizens and workers for lives in which they are entitled to nothing except what they can access through buying and selling (Sears and Cairns 2014). It does so through two main efforts, both of which are driven by currents of oppressive entitlement. First, Austerity U seeks to break young people's lingering expectations of publicly funded social services and the sense that people are entitled to secure, well-paying jobs and a retirement plan. Second, it fosters an entrepreneurial ethic that elevates labor market flexibility, consumer sovereignty, and individual economic resilience above democracy, equity, and public service. Austerity U orients students away from the state and toward the market for satisfying all needs and desires. In this vision, postsecondary schooling is not a public good, it is a commodity for purchase by consumers. By undercutting student expectations, Austerity U reflects and reproduces the legitimacy of the myth of the age of entitlement.

Making Austerity U means changing policies and ideas about what college education is, who is entitled to it, and what graduates can expect. Crucial efforts in the Austerity U project include ensuring mass student indebtedness, dehumanizing the learning process, and depoliticizing student life. To the extent that these and other efforts are achieved, millennial students are dispossessed of democratic entitlements won in earlier decades through struggles from below. The settle-for-less logic of the age of entitlement storyline is made to appear normal, an inevitable outcome of modern society. Building Austerity U widens economic inequality, deepens social exclusions, and works against the development of genuinely democratic, equitable postsecondary schooling.

SQUARELY IN THE RED

About 70 percent of graduates from public and private nonprofit colleges in the United States hold student debt. Between 2004 and 2014, the average debt held by grads rose 56 percent, from $18,550 to $28,950 (Institute for College Access & Success 2015). By 2014, student debt in the United States topped $1 trillion. Students are now among the most indebted cohorts in America—and student debt is one of the only types of debt that doesn't disappear as a result of filing for bankruptcy (Harris 2015). In Canada, the average university graduate leaves school with about $27,000 in student loans (Sagan 2014).

A sizable number of students graduate between $50,000 and $100,000 in the hole.

The massive rise in student debt is the predictable outcome of specific policy decisions. It follows years of government cuts to the postsecondary sector. In the United States, between 2004 and 2014, "the share of public college funding provided by states has declined (from 62 to 51%) while the portion students and families are asked to pay has increased (from 32 to 43%)" (Institute for College Access and Success 2015, 7). In the 1960s and 1970s, governments in Canada paid more than 90 percent of postsecondary costs. By the 1990s, government spending had dropped to 57 percent. "Higher tuition fees have replaced almost all of the lost government funding" (Canadian Federation of Students 2013). After adjusting for inflation, students in Ontario faced a 244 percent rise in tuition and other compulsory fees between 1990 and 2011. Tuition now pays for more than half of postsecondary costs in that province. In the United Kingdom, postsecondary tuition had been free until 1998. Students and their families must now purchase what was once a state entitlement. As education theorist Henry Giroux (2013, 21) writes, "Along with health care, public transportation, Medicare, food stamp programs for low-income children, and a host of other social protections, higher education is being defunded as part of a larger scheme to dismantle and privatize all public services, goods, and spheres."

Student loan systems are driven by the promise to investors of profiting from student debt. The combination creates a student debt crisis; no other outcome could be expected. Policymakers and pundits may fairly marvel at the sheer size of student debt—$1 trillion is a mind-bogglingly enormous sum. But they cannot in good faith claim to have expected that decades of neoliberal education policy would place young people anywhere other than squarely in the red.

The rising financial burden on students teaches them a great deal. As the costs of education increase, and the proportion covered by public programs is cut, students are taught that they can't count on public support to meet even their basic needs. For Serena, a 25-year-old graduate of UCLA, going to college meant dealing with a tuition hike every year: "A few weeks after I first arrived on campus, there was a tuition increase of 9 percent. And I was like … *Wait, what? I'm going to school because I thought I could actually afford it ... so what's all this about?"* (personal communication). In her sophomore year, tuition was hiked by 32 percent. She was forced to take on debt to finish her degree, but taking a student loan changed more than just her financial status. "Student loan debt shapes folks' worldview," she told me. "We were told that education is 'a ladder of opportunity.' But you take on all this debt and you realize, it's really a ladder to nowhere."

Genevieve LeBaron is a political theorist at the University of Sheffield in the United Kingdom. She urges us to think about debt as a tool for imposing discipline. Student debt can appear as though it's simply the fair outcome of an equitable agreement between consenting parties: No one forces millennials or their families to take out loans to pay for school. LeBaron (2014) challenges the notion that people freely choose to go into debt by drawing attention to the social contexts in which individuals make decisions.

Political and business leaders, as well as labor market trends, make it clear that anyone expecting even a basic living standard must go to college. In a context in which holding a degree is part of the new normal, it's problematic to say that students "choose" to go into debt the same way people choose to go into debt to buy a luxury car. Referring to the United States, Brooklyn-based journalist (and millennial) Malcolm Harris (2015) writes, "The economic choice this country poses to young people about higher education has stopped being about opportunity for wealth—now it's about fear of poverty." Between 1986 and 2013, people without a college education saw their real earnings drop $2,525.

The scale of the student loan industry further bolsters LeBaron's view of debt as a form of discipline. Debt is a relationship. Millions of students are going into debt in hopes of raising their chances at a good life. The incentives of creditors are different. Governments and private corporations make billions of dollars on interest from student loans. Banks, loan-servicing companies, and debt collectors are making staggering profits on student dispossession. In the words of Rohit Chopra, who worked for the US Consumer Financial Protection Bureau, "There is a large student loan industrial complex. Rising costs of college and flat family incomes have created enormous business opportunity for every step of the loan process" (in Lorin 2015).

For Generation Y, student debt is not an aberration; nor can student debt figures be ignored for being insignificant. A core part of being a student is leaving school owing tens of thousands of dollars. Serena observes that a highly indebted millennial workforce faces considerable pressure to take whatever jobs are on offer, on whatever terms employers feel like offering. "Having Nelnet or whatever loan provider you have sending you emails or calling you if you're late—and they call right away if you're late—it just feels like ... you're trying to get on your feet, but everybody's coming for you already" (personal communication). Young workers are often required to pay between $300 and $600 per month in loan-servicing fees. They have strong incentives to hustle from part-time job to part-time job and not complain about the low pay and no benefits at their workplace. Indebted people tend to have little time for political activism.

The neoliberal economy needs a disempowered workforce lacking a collective sense of entitlement to fairer employment conditions. Debt is disempowering. Becoming indebted is also risky. Accepting economic risk as a core responsibility of citizenship and working life is crucial to the second major component of the Austerity U reform project.

PRODUCING "INTRAPRENEURS"

As discussed in Chapter 3, the neoliberal economy extends and deepens precariousness across the working class. As "one of the world's leading management thinkers" puts it in the *Harvard Business Review*, "In a business, entitlement inhibits innovation" (Johnson 2012). Austerity U aims to transform the curriculum in all programs so that being a successful student involves embracing democratic disentitlement by developing the entrepreneurial spirit.

The *Oxford English Dictionary* (OED 2016b) defines an entrepreneur as someone "who undertakes an enterprise; one who owns and manages a business; a person who takes the risk of profit or loss." An introductory textbook on entrepreneurship says that people with the entrepreneurial spirit possess "resilience, tenacity [...] personal drive and ambition," as well as a knack for "risk taking," and applying "creativity and imagination" to "create and accumulate wealth" (Butler

2006, 13). Business schools have long taught entrepreneurship. The push to embed entrepreneurship at the core of PSE is to train the next generation of workers and citizens for lives of constant hustle, self-promotion, flexibility, high stress, uncertainty, and the absence of state and workplace benefits.

The vision is spelled out clearly in a report from the heads of Ontario universities: "At the core, [universities] are now developing an innovation capacity in students that will enable them to be 'intra-preneurs'—employees who behave like entrepreneurs within the con-text of a large organization" (Council of Ontario Universities 2013, 1). Intrapreneurs—students who embody the entrepreneurial ethic—are self-reliant, self-promotional, and resilient. They make sure to keep more than one option open, knowing that failure is always a strong possibility. They expect constant change; they don't rely on anything but their own gumption. They're constantly networking, individually responsible for making connections that may be financially useful down the road. They're optimistic and charismatic no matter what hardships they encounter.

Promoters of entrepreneurial education often cheer the "incuba-tors" and "launch pads" springing up across campuses everywhere. Official incubators aim to transform ideas generated by students and faculty into goods and services that can be sold on the market. For example, the university I teach at created the Laurier LaunchPad to facilitate student–faculty participation in business ventures on campus and in the surrounding community. Working through the LaunchPad, "students from all disciplines can earn a university course credit while creating profitable, scalable businesses" (Council of Ontario Universities 2013, 3). Democratic presidential candidate Hillary Clinton promised "would-be entrepreneurs" special student loan deferments (Lapowsky 2016).

It can seem as though entrepreneurial education is designed to make every graduate a Mark Zuckerberg. But the neoliberal economy doesn't need millions of inventers and CEOs of start-ups. In fact, if this were the only thing on offer, the system would immediately im-plode. An extremely small fraction of college graduates will go on to become heads of industry. Economist Michael Zweig (2006) estimates that the entire "ruling class" in America, which he defines as "those who give strategic direction to the country as a whole, extending beyond their own business or institution," could fit in Yankee Stadium's 54,000 seats. Add small business owners to this group, including those whose business isn't even their sole source of income, and you still end up with only around 10 percent of the population. A much smaller fraction of this small group will be the kinds of entrepreneurs profiled in university promotional material. *Forbes* reports that more than 90 percent of start-ups fail (Patel 2015). Most graduates will become neither inventors nor owners or managers (Fiedler 2015). They will become wage workers in an increasingly precarious labor market.

In an economy where unemployment is high (especially among youth), work is increasingly part time and temporary, and state entitlements have been slashed, new generations of workers need to have older expectations about job security and compensation crushed. Ideal intrapreneurial graduates of Austerity U enter the labor market prepared to piece together survival wages through a patchwork of low-paid, part-time work. Reorienting PSE around the entrepreneurial ethic encourages students to approach working life as an unstable, fierce competition in which success comes through the capacity to constantly sell oneself as being a flexible, self-motivated, and resilient hustler in the face of continuous hardship.

Employers still demand a disciplined workforce. But ideally, from the bosses' point of view, workers will become more and more *self-disciplined*. Think of the self-discipline required of Uber drivers who want to make enough money to buy food. They don't have a supervisor looking over their shoulder. The employment arrangement requires the entrepreneurial spirit. Think of retail workers at the mall who keep their jobs only if they learn to take on the identity of the brand they're selling. Think of the self-discipline needed for millennial interns to survive doing difficult work for little or no pay.

Studies by Kate Cairns (2012), a scholar of youth cultures, show that entrepreneurial education aims to create not only a particular kind of worker but a new generation of "entrepreneurial citizens" fit for a society based on the rule of the market. Entrepreneurial citizens are "not ruled through coercion" but are "invited to reap the benefits" of acting on their own behalf through savvy consumer decisions (46). They've got debt to pay off. Unemployment insurance is no longer an option. Pensions are a thing of the past. Yet the entrepreneurial citizen views indebtedness, constant hustle, financial risk taking, and other features of the age of austerity in a positive light. They view their individual creativity and cooperative capacities as marketable skills.

Policy analyst Eric Newstadt (2015) argues that over the next several years the overtly entrepreneurial programs on campuses—the incubators, launch pads, and tech-ecosystems explicitly designed to transform research into profit—"will operate as 'poles of adjustment.'" These poles will mark the new standards of excellence "around which every other taught program will be forced to articulate" and will prove their viability in the eyes of university administrators (163). As a result, learning in postsecondary institutions is being dehumanized. Education theorist Henry Giroux (2013, 17) writes that "the revamping of the curriculum to fit the interests of the market [...] not only contradicts the culture and democratic value of higher education but also makes a mockery of the very meaning and mission of the university as a place both to think and to provide the formative culture and agents that make a democracy possible."

THE MYTH OF THE AGE OF ENTITLEMENT GOES TO COLLEGE

In spite of neoliberal reforms, entrepreneurialism has not been fully internalized by all members of Gen Y. The ongoing refusal of students to lower their expectations to fit within the framework of neoliberal citizenship explains a third core trend of Austerity U: namely, an effort to delegitimize student demands for democracy and equality through a campus-specific version of the age of entitlement myth.

As the neoliberal university entitles students to less, more of what students request or expect can be framed as overly entitled. For example, *Globe and Mail* columnist Margaret Wente (2013) has repeatedly argued that postsecondary education in the millennial era is plagued by a student "expectations crisis." Today's students, she says, enroll in whatever program makes them feel good with no concern for industry needs. Each year, thousands of arts majors ignore the growing importance of the so-called STEM fields (science, technology, engineering, and math) and continue to dally in literature, history, women's studies, and other fields that aren't saleable on the job market. Arts grads whine about a tough employment scene. But, says Wente, it's their fault for not seeing it coming, for expecting something different.

In 2014, a front-page article in a major Canadian daily was headlined "I bought my degree, now I want my job!" Entitled students on fast track to becoming disgruntled employees" (Boesveld 2014). The study showcased in the article was conducted by Amy Peirone, a PhD student in sociology at the University of Windsor. Peirone's research described what she calls the growing problem of "academic entitlement." She characterized the problem by talking about students expecting good grades without having to work hard, "view[ing] their professors as employees," and demanding exceptional treatment. Sociologists James Cote and Anton Allahar (2007) blame this problem on grade inflation in the high school system. They worry about millennial blowback "when professors do not kowtow to pressures for easy grades from students who are accustomed to putting out little or no effort" (10). Cote and Allahar's framing of the problem as one of "an oversupply of 'unsorted' students with high expectations and unrealistic estimates of their own abilities" (42) feeds the myth of the age of entitlement.

The Atlantic's 2015 cover story "The Coddling of the American Mind" examined the supposed "oversensitivity of college students" today (Lukianoff and Haidt 2015). It was one of the magazine's most widely shared and hotly debated features that year. "The Millennials," wrote Greg Lukianoff and Jonathan Haidt (a constitutional lawyer and an academic, respectively), have been brought up by overprotective parents who have taught the lesson that "adults will do everything in their power to protect you from harm." As a result, Gen Y college students expect university professors and administrators to shelter them from ideas and experiences that may upset them.

Informed by the same assumptions, an opinion piece on CNN.com attacked students of color at Yale University for raising concerns about racist Halloween costumes on campus in 2015. Alex Castellanos (2015) ridiculed millennials for harboring "the idea that they are entitled to rich, full lives." He pooh-poohed student visions of greater social inclusiveness, warning that "the culture of entitlement in colleges" will produce a disastrously entitled citizenry. Unless the United States stops graduating students with "degrees in self-indulgence" it will end up a country where, God forbid, everyone is entitled to "a $15 minimum wage, our neighbors must pay for our health care, and our retirements are magically guaranteed."

According to *The Atlantic* article, the uniquely millennial dependence on "emotional reasoning" is what's driving student campaigns for campus safe spaces and requests for "trigger warnings" on course outlines that touch on potentially traumatic issues. It's all symptomatic of a generationally specific sense of being entitled not to be uncomfortable, a claim of the "right to not be offended." Actor and Academy Award–winning director Clint Eastwood used less decorous language when calling millennials part of "a pussy generation. Everybody's walking on eggshells. We see people accusing people of being racist and all kinds of stuff. When I grew up, those things weren't called racist" (in Mazza 2016). An article in the same vein in the *Daily Beast* concluded that millennials leave school "even less prepared to deal with anything approaching the real world" (Gillespie 2015). When students protested against racism on US campuses in late 2015, they were described as "overreacting, hysterical, entitled and coddled," accused of being "unable to grasp reality" (McClennen 2015).

Critics of trigger warnings and "the coddling of the American mind" portray themselves as being anti-entitlement. They assert that students are not entitled to shape the learning experience of everyone based on their individual sensitivities. In fact, these critics are deeply committed to defending entitlement in the classroom. It's just that they feel entitled to not have their own sensitivities triggered by marginalized voices challenging traditional curricula and forms of classroom conduct. Sara Ahmed (2014a) is a professor in race and cultural studies at the University of London. She writes that critics of trigger warnings treat them as "something that would get in the way of our freedom." But students who ask for warnings about traumatic material are asking "for more not less: asking for us to complicate the materials; to situate the materials; to consider how materials can create ripples in how they move us." Cultural critic Lindy West (2015) writes that "attending to the needs of students with PTSD [post-traumatic stress disorder] doesn't hinder academic freedom; it expands it."

The most effective use of trigger warnings and other ways of attending to historical and present injustices on campus will be worked out in practice among students and teachers (Godderis and Root

2016). Ahmed (2015) describes trigger warnings not as the primary means of achieving safety and openness on campus but "as a partial and necessarily inadequate measure to enable some people to stay in the room so that 'difficult issues' can be discussed." Addressing trauma in the classroom is a work in progress. The important point here is that critics of so-called entitled millennial students demonstrate a profound sense of entitlement to not have to deal with the trauma that many students who've experienced gendered violence, racism, and other forms of oppression have no choice but to deal with. The question is not, as the age of entitlement myth implies, whether we should let entitlement into the classroom or not. The question is whose experiences and feelings are entitled to be included and attended to in teaching and learning, and are we satisfied with the reasons why some continue to be excluded?

Promoting the entrepreneurial ethic as the gold standard of student identity across all fields provides the next generation with a framework for making sense of how to navigate life without a social safety net. And where even financial hardship and the invitation to imagine oneself as a savvy entrepreneur have failed to snuff out student demands for economic, political, or emotional support, the myth of the age of entitlement, tailored for campus, is at the disposal of those seeking to undercut student expectations.

"THE RENAISSANCE OF STUDENT ACTIVISM"

Austerity U has been consolidated since the Great Recession of 2008–09; yet as students in Quebec showed with inspiring strength and creativity, resistance to Austerity U persists. Postsecondary schooling reflects the needs of the dominant economy, but campuses are not strictly tools of ruling elites. As Bowles and Gintis (1976) observed in the 1970s, campuses are key battlegrounds for struggles between oppressive and democratic forces. Campuses are sites of social conflict because they're shot through with contradictions:

> On the one hand, employers and other social elites have
> sought to use the schools for the legitimation of inequality

through ostensibly meritocratic and rational mechanisms for allocating individuals to economic positions; they have sought to use the schools for the reproduction of profitable types of worker consciousness and behavior through a correspondence between the social relationships of education and those of economic life. On the other hand, parents, students, worker organizations, blacks, ethnic minorities, women, and others have sought to use schools for their own objectives: material security, culture, a more just distribution of economic reward, and a path of personal development conducive not to profits but to a fuller, happier life. (101)

In the millennial era, campus life is being restructured to serve the neoliberal economy; yet colleges and universities continue to foster tremendous democratic potential. And there is always the risk that the same sort of employer-friendly creativity, critical thinking skills, and teamwork capacities taught in Austerity U will be used by students and workers to press their own interests. The democratic imagination flourished in the student movements of the 1960s and 1970s; today, there are new signs of mass democratic awakenings on campuses.

A 2015 article in *The Atlantic* titled "The Renaissance of Student Activism" reported that "[a]t least 160 student protests took place in the U.S. over the course of the 2014 fall semester alone" (Wong 2015). This flowering of student opposition is happening as campaigns against Austerity U are transforming into fights against all forms of social inequality. Neoliberalism values only what has market value. Women's studies, ethnic studies, and labor studies programs are in constant danger of being shut down for being unmarketable. University administrations have attacked student campaigns for university divestment from corporations and states with dubious ecological and human rights records. Resisting the push from above to depoliticize campuses, the new student movements are driven by a vision of PSE rooted in social justice and equity. Both within and alongside campus struggles against tuition hikes and student debt, student movements against all forms of discrimination appear to be on the rise.

In one of the most highly publicized protests, Columbia University student Emma Sulkowicz carried a 50-pound mattress at all times when on campus between September 2014 and May 2015. Part protest, part performance art, Sulkowicz launched her "Mattress Performance (Carry that Weight)" with the demand that the university expel the male student against whom she'd made a formal accusation of raping her. Sulkowicz's demonstration lasted until her very final moments as a student: During graduation, she carried the mattress across the stage (Taylor 2015). Her protest tactic and the details of her experience generated debate on campuses and in the news media. Part of the reason Sulkowicz's specific protest attracted such attention was that it was launched in a campus context where the problem of violence against women is increasingly being openly talked about and struggled against.

A study by the US Department of Justice (2016) concludes that one in five women will be sexually assaulted during her years at postsecondary school. The student network Feminist Campus (2016) states that 43 percent of dating women on college campuses report experiencing physically or emotionally abusive dating behavior. My colleague at Wilfrid Laurier University, social work professor Ginette Lafrenière (2015), points out that in addition to addressing the issue of sexual violence on campus, "it is equally important to pay attention to defining the idea of 'gendered violence,' including cat calls, derogatory name calling, homophobic statements, and racial slurs. All of these practices and behaviors establish, exploit and reinforce gendered power-inequities that result in physical, sexual, emotional, economic or mental harm." In a society where sexism runs deep, millennial women and members of the LGBTQ community on campus face particular forms of gendered disentitlement.

Yet campuses are also a core organizing base of millennial feminist politics. Groups such as Columbia's "No Red Tape," which supported Sulkowicz's activism, offer visions of postsecondary education free of gendered discrimination. Students at Columbia University are pushing to have gender equity integrated into the core curriculum (Beccaro and Ganesh 2016). The survivor- and student-led organization Know Your IX (2016; which draws its name from the US law prohibiting sex discrimination on campus) "aims to empower students to end sexual and dating violence in their schools." Writers and organizers like Wagatwe Wanjuki (2014) highlight the need for millennial struggles against gendered violence to be actively anti-racist, anti-homophobic, and advocates of disability politics. This student-led vision of democratic entitlement on campus involves ending patriarchy, which millennial lawyer Jill Filipovic describes as an oppressive system allowing men to "feel entitled to dominate and control women's bodies" (in Friedman and Valenti 2008, 26). The fight against sexism is the fight for democratic entitlement.

Building on the strength of the Black Lives Matter movement off campus, students at Princeton University attracted national and international media coverage in fall 2015 with their campaign to rename the Woodrow Wilson School of Government (Wilson 2015). Woodrow Wilson was president of Princeton between 1902 and 1910 and president of the United States from 1913 to 1921. In the official curriculum taught in schools, he is also a hero of liberty and democracy, one of the founders of the League of Nations, a forerunner of the United Nations. However, Wilson was also openly racist, though this characteristic of his tends to be downplayed by his celebrants today. Wilson oversaw the deepening of segregation between whites and blacks within the federal government during his presidency (Keylor 2013).

Black students and their anti-racist allies demanded Wilson's name no longer serve as a symbol of their school's collective identity. Princeton should not have honored a person holding Wilson's racist views in the first place. As long as the school kept Wilson's name, exclusions were built into membership in the Princeton community, they argued. Students' histories and identities were being ignored or erased. Genuinely equitable campus citizenship cannot rely on markers rooted in oppressive entitlement.

Earlier the same month, a campaign led by black students at the University of Missouri forced the president of the school to resign after his administration failed to address longstanding concerns about the persistence of racism on campus. The student group leading the campaign to oust President Tim Wolfe called itself "Concerned Student 1950." The name recalls the year in which the University of Missouri admitted its first black student. In an interview on *Democracy Now* (2015), student activist Danielle Walker explained that the dramatic overthrow of President Wolfe was the result of years of organizing and outreach. Anti-racist student activists conducted research documenting the extent of the problem of racism on campus, held information sessions, forged coalitions with supportive faculty and other student groups, and repeatedly demanded answers and action from the president and his administration.

The struggle escalated on 3 November when graduate student Jonathan Butler went on hunger strike in support of the demands of Concerned Student 1950. Butler said that President Wolfe "had ample opportunity to create policies and reform that could shift the culture of Mizzou in a positive direction but in each scenario he failed to do so" (in Pearson 2015). Student protests and walkouts in support of Butler spread.

On 7 November, the campaign won the support of the Mizzou football team. A photograph posted on Twitter showed more than two dozen football players, many in Mizzou Tigers hoodies, linking arms with each other above the caption "We are no longer taking it. It's time to fight" (Legion of Black Collegians 2015). Butler, the hunger striker, stood in the center of the photo, linking arms with two players, surrounded by the rest of the team. A short statement accompanying the image read "The athletes of color on the University of Missouri football team truly believe 'Injustice Anywhere is a threat to Justice Everywhere.' We will no longer participate in any football related activities until President Tim Wolfe resigns or is removed due to his negligence toward marginalized students' experiences. WE ARE UNITED!!!!!" Less than 48 hours later, Tim Wolfe announced his resignation.

Sulcowicz, Mizzou students, strikers pinned with red squares—each addressed specific grievances using tactics developed to fit local contexts. All exemplify efforts to build solidarity in the name of expanding campus citizenship and making it more equitable. They clarify the links between building a more accessible, democratic postsecondary system and a society that nourishes robust social rights and democratic control not only in the political sphere but also in our workplaces, schools, and communities. They reject the settle-for-less logic of the age of entitlement narrative.

LA LUTTE CONTINUE

According to the myth of the age of entitlement on campus, PSE costs society too much and offers too little in return. It feeds millennial fantasies by letting masses of students study subjects with no obvious commercial value or industry fit. By promoting the "right not to be offended," college worsens millennial self-obsession, threatening the social order and creating overly entitled workers (Lukianoff and Haidt 2015). The new economy is high-tech and constantly changing. It requires flexible workers and savvy consumers. The postsecondary system is traditional, committed to structures and ideals that are out of touch with the new reality. The age of entitlement myth bolsters efforts to build Austerity U.

Contrary to the prevailing perspective, recent changes in postsecondary education have in fact *disentitled* students in various ways. Yet the strongest democratic currents opposing the entitlement framework underlying Austerity U do not take the form of demands to conserve the old system; rather, they are the transformative visions and actions of the new student movements. Like the architects and advocates of Austerity U, the new student movements assume that the status quo is unsustainable and undesirable. However, their vision of an alternative PSE system is fundamentally different. In the words of the manifesto of the Quebec student movement of 2012, equitable schooling "must banish all forms of gender-based discrimination" and end university complicity with "everyday racism," colonialism, and environmental destruction (CLASSE 2012). The manifesto explains that access to such a system "can only be equal if it is free," for "where there is free access, we *share* payment for *shared* services."

The organizations of the Quebec student movement recognized that a free, equitable, and democratically run postsecondary education system will only be achievable when egalitarianism and direct democracy spread through all areas of society. Their manifesto notes that students depend on the power drawn from social movements off campus, especially those led by Indigenous peoples, who have "kept up the fight" against economic and environmental exploitation. In other words, the manifesto envisions a feedback loop of popular power: the mutual reinforcement of struggles for democratic education, Indigenous rights, public services, environmental justice, and gender and sexual liberation. "This is the meaning of our vision, and the essence of our strike: it is a shared, collective action whose scope lies well beyond student interests."

If we reject the core assumption of the myth of the age of entitlement—the idea that "young people should settle for less"—and we are curious about the possibility of a world in which people are entitled to have their core needs met, we can learn a lot and draw considerable hope from millennial student movements. Postsecondary education is central to the millennial condition. Whether it will authorize and fuel currents of oppressive entitlement or help usher in a new era of democratic entitlements is an open question. Answers depend on the extent to which the new student movements are able to grow and cohere and fight for a system of higher education devoted to meeting human needs.

CHAPTER FIVE

MILLENNIAL BLOWOUT: ECO-DISENTITLEMENT VERSUS ECOLOGICAL JUSTICE

MILLENNIAL MELTDOWN

Leading climate scientists warn of imminent ecological collapse. A 2014 report from the United Nations says that life as we know it will not be possible after average global temperatures rise four degrees Celsius, which "is more likely than not" going to happen in the next 80 years (Intergovernmental Panel on Climate Change 2014, 19). Even the pope recognizes the "very solid scientific consensus" showing "a disturbing warming of the climatic system" (Pope Francis 2015). Young people's health and relationship to nature is threatened by climate change caused by industrial development, and "climate change will have a significant impact on millennials' household incomes and wealth, with rapidly worsening effects by mid-century, as the youngest millennials reach their peak earning years" (NextGen Climate and Demos 2016). Yet self-declared experts on Generation Y continue to talk as if the real problem with young people today is that they aren't grateful enough for the lavish spread of luxuries and opportunities all around. The planet is burning, and millennials are told to lower their expectations. The myth of the age of entitlement ignores the environmental crisis facing Gen Y.

Existing political and economic institutions do not entitle millennials to a healthy environment. When functioning properly, these institutions ensure that millennials are *disentitled* to one. The ways of producing and consuming goods and services that are now not merely the norm but are actively promoted by governments and industry have led to "desertification, deforestation, soil depletion, and the ever-present possibility of nuclear warfare" (Williams 2010, 4). The world millennials inhabit is one of ocean acidification, the melting of glaciers (which is both a symptom and cause of global warming), rising sea levels, and increasingly frequent and intense "extreme weather events." Climate change researcher Chris Williams (2010, 3) sums up our predicament chillingly: "if humanity continues on its present course [...] civilization on anything like the current scale cannot be sustained." Government proclamations, nongovernmental organization (NGO) visioning documents, and well-meaning community leaders assert that *everyone is entitled to a healthy environment.* In fact, the ecological basis necessary for the reproduction of the human species is being unsustainably undercut by business as usual.

This is hardly news to millennials. In the late 1980s, when I belted out songs during my elementary school's production of "Assignment: Earth, What Kids Can Do to Save the Planet," it was still something of a novelty for a major school project to focus on the threat of environmental disaster. By the early 2000s, though, green curriculum was standard fare. Today virtually every school in the Western world teaches kids about the dangers of global warming. Much is made about the importance of reducing, reusing, and recycling. If Gen Y is symbolized by Facebook, Harry Potter, and UGG boots, so too is its story told by pictures of clear-cut forests, nuclear meltdowns, and the Gulf of Mexico drowned in oil.

The severity of environmental degradation is widely recognized as a problem, especially by younger people who've grown up with eco-panic as part of the furniture in the room. Millennials have good reason to be furious about the state they're in. They'd be justified in demanding radical new social rights and democratic control over the economy that would turn the ideal of being entitled to environmental sustainability into reality. There are indeed large numbers of young environmental activists. However, broadly speaking, Gen Y's orientation to the environmental crisis is not defined by a vibrant sense of deserving these sorts of essential changes. Many millennials, including those on the frontlines of the ecological crisis, feel entitled to very little when it comes to a healthy environment for themselves and their children.

This chapter takes an up-close look at struggles over ecological entitlements. It focuses on the experiences and ideas of young people in communities near the Gulf of Mexico in the United States. The case study helps us think about the complex, often contradictory relationship between young people and environmental crises. The same millennials who love their natural surroundings and fear ecological catastrophe also depend on and identify with industries that are among the worst offenders against ecological sustainability.

The everyday ecological disentitlement of millennials is so deeply rooted and sprawling it can seem normal. It can feel impossible to imagine a future in which people are entitled to ecological sustainability. But environmental organizations and campaigns, many of which are powered by millennials, are imagining just such a world and working to make it real. In North America, Indigenous youth are at the forefront of movements that frame democracy and ecological sustainability as inseparable. Millennial-led environmental movements expand our sense of democratic entitlement to include ecological justice. This is a radical challenge to political and economic traditions that assume you can have true freedom and democracy while destroying life on Earth. It rejects the neoliberal vision of society in which environmental security is available only to those who can pay for it.

DISASTER SURVIVALISM

Millennial resignation to environmental collapse struck me with special force while talking with high school students in New Orleans, Louisiana, at the annual SHOREline Summit in May 2015. SHOREline is a "youth empowerment project" involving students in high schools across the Gulf of Mexico region in the United States— Texas, Louisiana, Alabama, Mississippi, and Florida (National Center for Disaster Preparedness 2016b). Student volunteers in SHOREline work with peers in their high school on a year-long project responding to environmental disasters. Student leadership is highly valued in the program. Each SHOREline chapter is supervised by a teacher, but students are the ones who choose and manage the projects.

The program was launched in 2013 by two university professors. Their research drew attention to the effects of environmental disasters on young people in states bordering the Gulf of Mexico. Young people in that region "have been *exposed* to more disasters over the past decade than any other group of young people" in the United States (National Center for Disaster Preparedness 2016a). The Gulf Coast was ground zero for two of the most devastating environmental disasters of the century: Hurricane Katrina (2005) and the British Petroleum oil spill (2010). Studies conclude that the effects of these disasters—the loss of lives, housing, schools, and industries—together with the constant threat of future environmental catastrophes, have "led to an *accumulation* of mental and physical health issues and educational and social challenges" among youth in Gulf communities (ibid.)

At the end of the school year, SHOREliners from all participating high schools gather for a two-day summit in a large auditorium at the University of New Orleans. On presentation Saturday, they dress in business casual: boys in khaki slacks and oversized dress shirts; girls in dresses and little sweaters to protect their shoulders from the room's aggressive air conditioning. On team-building Sunday, everyone is in matching mustard-yellow SHOREline T-shirts. On the last two days of May 2015, I too donned slacks and a sports jacket, despite the New Orleans heat. I went to the summit to learn what problems and solutions were on the minds of these ecologically concerned teens living within an ecological danger zone. I wanted to find out whether they felt entitled to a better environmental future.

The chapter from Gulfport High School, located in Mississippi, unveiled its "Project Clean Space" in a homemade promotional video. Students from Gulfport had designed "a program intended to distribute disaster kits attending to the sanitary needs of homeless youth" in case of an evacuation order.[11] The kit, a gray plastic backpack-sized

---

11 All direct quotations from the SHOREline Summit are drawn from my audio recordings of the proceedings and materials distributed by the conference organizers.

capsule filled with sanitary wipes, bandages, deodorant, and tooth-paste, was also meant to serve as a portable washing machine. The video showed Kyla modeling a "Project Clean Space" T-shirt while sliding down a bannister in Gulfport High. SHOREliners in the audience hooted with delight. On the screen, Kyla pretended to be a great scientist while stirring water and laundry detergent in the capsule.

The five SHOREliners from South Lafourche High School, which sits on Bayou Lafourche in southern Louisiana, reported on their col-lection of disaster-related "life hacks." Life hacks is an Internet-era term for repurposing everyday items to meet a different need than the one they were designed to meet. This presentation also began with a bit of fun: a wide-eyed blonde student cheerfully called into the microphone: "Hey! Did y'all know that you can burn Doritos? They can start a fire!" South Lafourche's actual burning of Doritos (and crayons, which, it turns out, work well as do-it-yourself candles) made their exhibition table by far the most photographed.

Students from the rural community of Thibodaux, Louisiana, told of their park beautification project. While they were no less enthu-siastic about their work, the three students representing this chapter spoke softly into the microphone. Chantelle later told me she dreamt of writing a book about "growing up in the ghetto." During the presentation, she expressed hope that the murals and play structures they'd installed in a local park would serve two functions. Most im-portant, they would be a meeting place in the aftermath of a disaster. But they'd also serve as fertile ground upon which people could gather and get to know each other, thus building community resilience be-fore disaster strikes.

All six of the projects presented at the summit were similarly creative, smart, and driven by a sense of civic engagement. But like those of the Gulfport, South Lafourche, and Thibodaux chapters, all also accepted without question that environmental disasters are here to stay. Three projects focused on providing immediate relief in the event of an emergency. Three focused on ways either to prepare for an emergency or deal with its longer-term effects. No teen raised the possibility of changing our relationship with the environment in ways that might lead to a disaster-free (or even disaster-lite) future. There was no talk of being entitled to eco-justice; no demand for local control over environmentally damaging industries.

SHOREline's focus is disaster response, and the program emphasizes the value of practicability. Yet, in light of all that's known about the ecologically damaging effects of industrial production, I'd expected to hear more ideas involving more ambitious political and economic transformation. SHOREline is composed of environmentally conscious, civically oriented teenagers. There might reasonably have been at least a few projects geared more toward transforming how we interact with the environment and less on merely surviving eco-disasters through individual ingenuity and new consumer products. Instead, these students appeared resigned to lives of "disasters as usual."

I was especially surprised not to see a bolder vision from the students from South Lafourche. Their school sits within a hundred miles of where the British Petroleum (BP) oil well blowout occurred in 2010, a disaster that was reenacted in *Deepwater Horizon*, the 2016 Hollywood film starring Mark Wahlberg and Kate Hudson. On 20 April 2010, 11 workers on the Deepwater Horizon drilling rig were killed when oil ripped through the machinery designed to regulate its flow. The blowout shot oil from deep in the earth through thousands of feet of piping and into the air above the rig. Coating the deck and the men in its path, the oil quickly burst into flames. The fire and ensuing destruction injured 16 other workers. The entire rig sank two days later. The blowout ruined the capping and piping systems BP used to control the movement of oil from the mouth of the well on the seabed to the company's rig atop the water. With the well now open but not capped, thousands of barrels of oil were gushing uncontrollably into the sea.

Before traveling to New Orleans, I'd come across piles of evidence showing how the blowout devastated the region. In the documentary *Offshore*, Darla Rooks, a shrimper from Port Sulphur, Louisiana, says "We're catching ten per cent of what we're supposed to be catching. We can't survive; we can't pay our bills" (in Longfellow, Richards, and Helios Design Labs 2013). Dr. Samantha Joye, a lead researcher on the effects of the blowout, reported finding massive clouds (called "plumes") of oil and natural gas lurking thousands of feet underwater. She described these plumes as "3 to 5 kilometers wide and 10 to 20 kilometers long. Plus, they moved! They traveled at a speed of about three kilometers a day," killing sea life and wrecking the Gulf ecosystem along the way (in Dreifus 2011). Antonia Juhasz (2010, 101), biographer of the BP blowout, concluded that the nearly 2 million gallons of chemical dispersants BP sprayed on the Gulf after the spill created an "oil-and-dispersant toxic goo, multiplying the reach and the effect of both by an incalculable amount." Even beyond the 87 days oil spewed from the well into the water, all along the Gulf Coast people reported suffering from headaches, itchy eyes, and sneezing. A study published in the *Journal of the American Medical Association* in September 2010 concluded that the spill posed "direct threats to human health," either by breathing or touching oil or the dispersant chemicals BP had pumped into the sea (Solomon and Janssen 2010, 1118).

Why did none of this figure into the South Lafourche SHOREline project? Over dinner on Saturday night, I asked students from the community if they had experienced the impact of the BP blowout. Right away Lexi thrust the screen of her iPhone over her lasagna and into my hands. She told me to look at her grandparents' fishing camp. The video was shot from a camera held just above the water from the front of a small moving boat. The water was calm and looked muddy. Banks of low green reeds lined both sides of the screen. As I began remarking on the remote beauty of the landscape (prompting two others at the table to pull out their phones and begin looking for even more beautiful pictures to show me), Lexi recalled traveling to the fishing camp for the first time after the blowout: "All the fish and wildlife were dead," she said. "It took years to like ... yeah ... and it's still not like what it was before." Before Lexi finished her thought, Jessica, at my right, and Lindsay, at my left, spoke as though in stereo: "It's not like it was before / No goin' to the beach," they said at the same time. Their teacher, Ronda Wilson, sat across from me. Ronda wears rectangular glasses and holds a master's degree in marine biology. She told the students that when the BP oil spill happened, they were the same age she was when the World Trade Center was attacked on 11 September 2001. The students all nodded, as though the comparison between the two events was obvious. It took me a moment to understand: The spill is the shared collective reference point in the lives of these teens. Heather, the first to speak during the presentation earlier in the day, dropped her chin slightly while pointing a fork at me and said: "Well, now you know. That's our life."

They acknowledged seeing irony in the fact that many young people who would've been shrimpers and fishers are now more likely to end up working on the very oil rigs that threaten what's left of the community's seafood industry and fishing culture. But they scoffed at the idea that offshore oil drilling could be slowed, to say nothing of wound down in the name of environmental sustainability. "That's just how it *is*," Heather declared, her regional drawl giving the word "is" an extra syllable.

ECO-COMMUNITY THREATS AND HOPES IN SOUTH LAFOURCHE

It's an hour-and-a-half drive from the SHOREline Summit to South Lafourche. Moving south along the highways and backroads between New Orleans and Galliano, Heather reflected to herself: "You know … *I'm blessed*. I come from a place where everyone is a family. We have so much. We may not have a bowling alley, and we don't have a movie theater, but we have a lot of recreational crabbing and fishing, and, just, our culture itself is so unique. On that ride home, once I saw the bayou, I thought, *wow*—we're different!"

I spent a week in Heather's home town in July 2015. She and her fellow SHOREliners offered personalized tours and introductions to people "down the bayou," as everyone there says. Not much time is needed in South Lafourche to see the truth in Heather's post-summit reflections. The visual landscape and cultural norms *are* different; especially if you've grown up in small-town Ontario and now live in Toronto, one of North America's largest cities.

Bayou Lafourche is a 106-mile long, relatively narrow body of water that flows from the Mississippi River into the Gulf of Mexico. Driving down Highway 1, 45 minutes south of New Orleans, just past where Bayou Lafourche is bisected by the Intracoastal Waterway (which runs east–west between Texas and Florida), you come upon a string of towns running along the bayou: Larose, Cut Off, Galliano,

Golden Meadow, down to Leeville, and finally into Port Fourchon, which opens onto the Gulf just west of the last major piece of coastal land, Grand Isle. It's obvious why locals call Bayou Lafourche "the longest Main Street in the world" (Buskey 2010). Unlike cities whose rivers over time have become more decorative than functional, these communities are centered on the bayou, both culturally and geographically.

From a bird's-eye view, each town resembles a long centipede. The bayou is the body, the nerve center holding everything together. Jutting out from it on both sides (the creature's little legs) are roadways and laneways lined with trailers, bungalows, and hand-painted chipboard signs telling drivers to slow down or advertising the price for a bag of fresh crabs. Bayou Lafourche runs the full (north–south) few miles of each town; but the typical residential "street" running perpendicular to the water rarely reaches more than a half-mile before stopping abruptly at black and yellow dead end signs. Go another half-mile past the end of these residential laneways (which a few unmarked roadways do) and you'll run into 13-foot-tall levees—ridges of dirt and grass. The levees edging the towns protect them from flooding by the endless water in marshlands all around.

The bakeries, banks, churches, and motels in the towns of South Lafourche sit on the same stretch of bayou-lined road, less than 100 feet from the water. This bayou roadway is home, too, to boat-repair shops, hardware stores, and small aluminum-sided houses. South Lafourche High School (SLHS), the home of Heather's SHOREline chapter, is similarly no more than a hundred yards from the water. Although it's located in the town of Galliano, the northern border with Cut Off is only a mile and a half away, and the difference between the towns is unnoticeable except for the small sign marking it.

Where the bayou flows past SLHS, the waterway is about 175 feet wide. This allows for more than enough room to house the dozens of trawl boats, some of which are more than 80 feet long, docked on both sides all the way down Bayou Lafourche. Galliano's retractable bridge that crosses the bayou can get out of the way of a barge or a boat and return to carrying auto and foot traffic over the water in only a few changes of a streetlight. There are gas stations, a few trailers converted into restaurants, and a Walmart along Highway 3235, which runs parallel to Bayou Lafourche and which locals call "the backroad" or "the new highway." (It was built in 1984.) The backroad is less than a mile from the middle of town but feels far from life at the center.

During my time in South Lafourche, virtually every millennial I met echoed Heather's pride in community and love of the natural environment. "We do things nowheres else does," said Patrick, a recent graduate of SLHS, preparing to start college with dreams of becoming an anesthesiologist.[12] "Like, our school has a pirogue race," he said, referring to the small, canoe-like boats that hang in one of the town's historical exhibitions. "We go in the bayou and race during homecoming week. And that won't happen anywheres else." The main annual fundraiser for the SLHS cheerleading team is a day-long fishing rodeo on Grand Isle. Wearing matching purple T-shirts made especially for the day and makeup that ran in the 90°F heat, cheerleaders wrote down the weights of enormous fish on a white leader board. They served "pastalaya" (a pasta version of the Cajun delicacy jambalaya) to hundreds of parents and community supporters. Cheerleaders sang along to top-40 country hits and put elastic bands on crab claws to keep the creatures from clipping the children encircling the crab races.

Over eggs at Rose's Café on the backroad, wearing a striped tank-top, short hair, and a wide smile, Gilbert laughed when he asked "How many places you know that you walk straight outta ya house, you drop line, and catch fish, OK? I rode a jet ski to school on the last day. You know how many people I've told about that? I went to Lafayette and told them, and they said, 'Where you got water near yo school?' I said, on the bayou. They said, 'What's a bayou?'" In his SLHS Class of 2015 valedictory address, Gilbert rejected the idea that you have to move away to succeed. Looking down at his phone, he read a short section of his speech: "Look around. If there isn't happiness on this bayou, then why do people stay? This is where some of us, our families, have been rooted for decades. There are second- and third-generation graduates among us tonight."

---

12 All direct quotations and observations in this section are drawn from audio recordings and written notes I made in Louisiana between 17–21 July 2015 unless otherwise noted.

Standing atop the levee near the border of Galliano and Golden Meadow, her back to the center of town, Heather pointed to the wetlands stretching as far as could be seen. "That is my happy place back there," she said. This was the main destination on Heather's tour of South Lafourche. On the town side of the embankment stood a "Warning: Alligators" sign next to a small canal. Looking over the wetlands, Heather continued: "I love just riding around in the boat; especially with my dad. It's so peaceful back there." Shielding her eyes from the white almost-noon sunlight, then wiping sweat from her cheek, she recalled one especially fond memory of a night with friends at this very same spot: "We packed some snacks and we came right here and watched the sun set. And it was just … so beautiful!"

But Heather's reason for pointing to the scenery from atop Galliano's levees was not only to showcase the region's beauty and emphasize its centrality to the region's culture. She also wanted to warn of the imminent disaster facing people in her community. "We're slowly and surely sinking," she said. "They say that we're going to be gone in 50 years. But actually, it's going to be sooner. They say that Louisiana loses land—the coast of Louisiana loses about a football field of land" [*Jessica, who was co-guiding the tour, suddenly cut in: "every hour"*] "… every hour," said Heather. "Which, in y'all kind of terms [*translating the image for my Canadian imagination*] would be, maybe a soccer field? It's bad. We're disappearing, basically." Jessica spoke up again: "It's terrifying." And Heather went on: "It's sad. It's sad because, this is where we grew up; we would go to the park, we would go fishing. There's so many people here that we know and we love … we care about our home. And to see it slowly dying and disappearing, it's scary. It's scary and it's sad."

Ask anyone in the area, and they can probably provide you some version of the football field statistic. At breakfast, Gilbert, the valedictorian, said "we lose a football field of land every … something … day? Maybe month? No, I think it's day." An organizer at the fishing rodeo told me "it's every minute. One football field of land every minute." At the library, Shawn, a 27-year-old college student as well as a member of the United Houma Nation, said, "I think every day we lose, ah, I think it's like a football field—of land—every day."

An article in *Scientific American* confirms that the most accurate version is also one of the scariest: Southern Louisiana "is washing away at a rate of a football field every hour, 16 square miles per year" (Marshall 2014).

Why is South Lafourche disappearing? I asked Toby Rutherford of the Gulf Restoration Network. First, land is being eroded as saltwater from the Gulf enters the freshwater wetlands. Saltwater eats away at the sands, grasses, and marshy areas, dissolving the shoreline and swallowing islands throughout the region. This is happening so quickly that even millennials have observed the landscape transform. "Every time I go down [to Grand Isle]," said Heather, "there's less and less land. It's very upsetting."

Saltwater has always eroded parts of the coast, but the process is accelerating because of human production in the industrial era. For example, damming the Mississippi River prevents natural flood waters from redistributing restorative minerals and land deposits. The oil industry's building of canals to service wells both in- and offshore has opened up new passageways for saltwater to reach inland. A US government report estimates that oil and gas canals are responsible for up to 60 percent of land loss (Marshall 2014).

Toby Rutherford's account was repeated by Ronda Wilson, the leader of SLHS's SHOREline chapter and the school's ecology teacher. Ronda explained that oil extraction—not just the disruption caused by heavy transportation and drilling in the area, but the actual removal of oil from under the ocean—exacerbates the problem of soil erosion. While fixing a ceiling fan on her kitchen table, Ronda said that "coastal areas don't have any bedrock. So when they pump in the brine to push the oil up ... when we're pulling fluids out from underneath ... there's nothing left stabilizing it up top."

Studies show a correlation between areas where the most oil and gas have been extracted and areas where the worst soil erosion has occurred. Even a small amount of compression resulting from the weight of the ocean pressing on this weaker foundation can draw Louisiana's coast further into the Gulf. This is to say nothing of the corrosive effects of hurricanes and rising sea levels, which appear to be increasing in number and becoming more destructive as a result of global warming, which has been caused in large degree by society's dependence on fossil fuels. Turning back toward town on top of the levee, Heather said, "to think that this could all be gone with one more hurricane ... that's a scary thought."

Shawn, who so much loves "food and family," also talked about the BP spill's effects on traditional fishing and shrimping. He said that shrimper friends have told him that "they're seeing more and more females with no eggs" and "there's some shrimp with no eyes." He recently volunteered to participate in a Louisiana State University study on the spill's impact on human health. He recalls being terrified in the summer of 2010, when the spill was out of control: "They went down and found this fountain. And it wouldn't stop. It was like Old Faithful down there: just pumping oil, pumping oil, pumping oil. It was like, 10 days, 20 days, 50 days, 70 days ... and it was like ... [it] wouldn't even stop. Wouldn't. Even. Stop." He rejects the idea that the negative effects of the spill are over. "You hear them say 'it's OK.' I'm saying, 'No, it's not OK. It's not.' It's not short term; it's long term. [...] Look at the *Exxon Valdez* [the 1989 spill off the Alaskan coast that's still being cleaned up]. This is probably going to be a lifetime."

Yet in spite of his concerns about the effects of fossil fuel extraction in the region, Shawn is not opposed to the oil industry. This is partially because his father is a long-time production operator on an offshore rig. Shawn's family depends on a paycheck from a large oil company. But even when this direct connection is put to one side, Shawn has "mixed feelings" about oil production on the Gulf Coast, "because over here, the oil industry and native shrimping and trawling ... they're just ... tied together." To make his point, he describes an image designed by a member of the Houma Nation named Louise Billiot: "It's the image of a boat—half of it is a sunrise and a sunset—and then you have two triangles, and that represents the oil derricks."

Heather's dad works on a supply boat that serves the oil industry offshore. Gilbert's dad makes a living using a trawl boat to clear sections of the ocean floor when offshore sites are being bought or sold. Crystal, whose 34-pounder placed her first in the bull red category at the cheerleaders' fishing rodeo, was sorry her husband wasn't back from his 27-day offshore shift to share in her celebration. The Cajun Inn Motel, where I stayed, promotes itself online as being "perfect for working crews." The largest billboards on the backroad advertise lawyers specializing in offshore work-place injuries.

Two staff members at a kids' day camp at the Bayou Civic Club in Larose, both recent SLHS grads, began speaking at the same time when asked if they know anyone who works in the industry: "My dad," said Pam. "He's a driller on the rigs." After Pam finished, Patrick smiled shyly and spoke softly, as though embarrassed for not being more original: "My dad too ... inshore, on the machines. A lot of my family works in the industries," he continued. "All my uncles. We have a lot of oil in our family." Patrick's boss, Teresa Bertrim, the executive director of the Bayou Civic Club, spoke proudly of the fact that Patrick has family in Halliburton's Houston office. (Halliburton is a major contractor in the offshore oil industry and one of the companies found at fault for the BP oil spill.)

Teresa explained that people in South Lafourche embrace the oil industry because "we see it as a source of income. Not that we aren't aware of the physical aspects of what it does." She said she knows that kids are taught "how many football fields of land we lose each year because of erosion." But ultimately, she explained, "for us, it's really bread and butter. Like, even for us [referring to staff at the Bayou Civic Club], my big sponsors are Chevron, Shell, BP, Exxon Mobile. So, while they're taking from our community in an environmental aspect, they're giving back to the places where our kids grow up."

The biggest fear of millennials in South Lafourche is not another BP-like spill—it's the loss of jobs in the oil fields. Heather said her community is in constant fear of oil prices crashing:

> It's very scary. A lot of people are trying to find other jobs, and it's really hard. Because the oil field, that's all we really are. So what are these kids going to do? That just came up into my mind. I know a lot of kids that just graduated: They're not going to college. They're going to go to some boat-tech training school down here. What's going to happen to them just starting off?

At breakfast at Rose's Café, Lexi, one of the SLHS SHOREliners, asked Gilbert how the debris his trawl boat picks up from the ocean floor gets there in the first place. "You know the wells and all that?" Gilbert asked. "Well, this stuff," he said, pointing to pictures on his phone of recovered tires, piping, and enormous grates, "it'll fall off." There was a silent pause before Lexi and her friend laughed uncertainly. Does finding this "stuff" covering the ocean floor worry Gilbert? "I can't say it makes me happy. But, I mean ..." The economic tradeoff goes without saying. Just as it does when Lexi, after describing how "trash and chemicals" end up in the bayou because of northern pollution in the Mississippi River says, "It'd be nice to have the bayou a beautiful blue, and you could see the fish ... It'd be nice to have crystal blue water ... but we don't." Her desire for ecological health is not accompanied by a sense that such a thing is actually possible.

In the eyes of young people in South Lafourche, environmental disentitlement is the new normal. The oil industry is understood to be a fixture of the region, and many millennials and their loved ones depend on it for jobs, community resources, and a sense of purpose. In 2011, more than 20 percent of jobs in Golden Meadow were directly related to oil and gas production. A much higher percentage is indirectly related (Magill 2011). In light of their dependence on the fossil fuel industry, it was easier to see the reasoning behind South Lafourche's SHOREline disaster life hacks project. When virtually everything in their lives—material possessions, a sense of pride, career options—depends on the success of big oil, and in the absence of any real alternative to non–oil field economic success, there is fairly compelling logic to trading ecological sustainability for some degree of short-term economic stability.

If environmental degradation is understood to be an unstoppable force, it is unrealistic, if not absurd, to feel entitled to environmental health. And when the horizon of possibility does not stretch beyond a world without oil production, you know there will be more oil spills in the future and more extreme weather as the fossil fuel industry pumps more and more carbon dioxide into the atmosphere. Within this context of being routinely disentitled to environmental sustainability, developing consumer-based survival strategies is not just a good idea—it can appear to be the *only* idea.

ECO-ENTITLEMENT IN THE MILLENNIAL ERA

Over the past decade, members of the Northern Cheyenne Reservation in southeastern Montana have transformed dozens of homes in their community from being powered by coal to being powered by solar energy. Writer and activist Naomi Klein (2014, 395) explains that not only have household electricity bills been cut in half, but the boom in solar-related jobs has created new career opportunities for "young Cheyenne men who had spent time working in the coal industry and were tired of suppressing core parts of their identity to earn a paycheck."

The community ensured that the shift to renewables was done by community members who received skills training as part of the ecological project. Klein does not downplay the fact that the project required funding from the federal government's Environmental Protection Agency and NGOs. On the contrary, she emphasizes that ecological sustainability depends on massive new government investments in renewable energy, public transportation, health care, and other social services. It depends on the radical expansion of social rights and greater democratic control over the economy. In her words, "the measures we must take to secure a just, equitable, and inspiring transition away from fossil fuels clash directly with our reigning economic orthodoxy at every level" (94). It will take an incredible surge of democratic entitlements, at both the legal and emotional level, to meet the challenges of the climate crisis. Klein envisions a seismic shift in policies and actions that breaks deeply rooted economic and social patterns and "breaks all the ideological rules":

> [I]t requires visionary long-term planning, tough regulation of business, higher levels of taxation for the affluent, big public sector expenditure, and in many cases reversals of core privatizations in order to give communities the power to make the changes they desire. In short, it means changing everything about how we think about the economy so that our pollution doesn't change everything about our physical world. (Klein 2014, 83)

Klein argues that the threat of poverty is what keeps so many people dependent on jobs that hurt the environment. People wouldn't work at these jobs if they weren't forced to because they lack alternatives. She points to the example of Jeff King of the Northern Cheyenne. Once the renewable energy industry became a reality in his community, he was able to quit his coal job and start a business in solar power. What might the people of South Lafourche choose to do if their households didn't depend on jobs in the oil field? Love and respect for the environment is part of the region's sense of community. It's hard to imagine people would choose environmentally destructive jobs, goods, and services, if they were entitled to sustainable alternatives.

In April 2015, students at Harvard University in Cambridge, Massachusetts, blockaded a busy campus building for six days (Delwiche and Klein 2015). The action was part of "Heat Week" protests, organized by a group called "Divest Harvard." Founded in 2012, Divest Harvard demands that the university immediately withdraw all its direct investments from the top 200 fossil fuel companies on the stock market (valued at US$19.6 million in August 2015) and immediately freeze any new investments in fossil fuel companies. Further, it demands that the university divest all indirect holdings from fossil fuel companies within five years. In the words of Divest Harvard: "Higher education institutions like Harvard exist as investments in the future for their students and their countries. Yet, while investing in our future, Harvard simultaneously invests its $36.4 billion endowment—the largest University endowment in the world—in corporations that threaten our future and that of our planet by causing the climate crisis" (Divest Harvard 2016).

Divest Harvard's campaign expresses an audacious sense of entitlement to ecological sustainability. It imagines a world in which people's need for, and responsibility for maintaining, a healthy natural environment is fundamental to how our economics, politics, and all other parts of social life are organized. It also embraces what Klein (2014, 354) calls the "special moral authority" young people have in demanding ecological justice from postsecondary institutions. Colleges and universities, she says, invite young people to find wisdom and guidance within them, "so it is the height of hypocrisy for those same institutions to profit from an industry that has declared war on the future at the most elemental level."

Divest Harvard has been attacked by defenders of business as usual. Writing in the *Guardian*, financial advisor Heather Long (2013) told Divest Harvard to drop its dreaming because "large-scale divestment is completely unrealistic in today's global marketplace." In his book *How to Think Seriously about the Planet*, the British philosopher Roger Scruton (2012) dismisses high-profile champions of the environment as extremists. He rejects calls for sweeping environmental regulations that would coordinate social action to facilitate ecological sustainability, arguing all that's needed for ecological health is renewed individual commitments to friendship, civic honor, and local preservation. In an article attacking new environmental regulations emerging out of the Environmental Protection Agency, professor Steven Hayward (2015) says the US government agency has "become captive to ideological interest groups." He suggests that contrary to the EPA's responsibility to act on behalf of everyone, it has "for practical purposes become a wholly owned subsidiary of the environmental movement." Critics of the environmental movement frame it as a "special interest group" driven by unreasonable expectations of what policies can be changed and by how much.

These critics assume that neoliberal economic and political institutions are the limits within which any efforts at environmental protection must occur. Accepting the logic of market rule, it's assumed that change is made through individual consumer choices. When debate is organized by this assumption, demands for more fundamental policy and social change can easily appear or be made to seem "special" in the bad sense: reflective and productive of oppressive senses of entitlement. The precise language of "millennial entitlement" may not be as prevalent in debates over the sort of environmental stewardship we deserve (as opposed to debates about workplaces or campuses, in which the term is central), but the *settle-for-less* logic that structures the age of entitlement myth in other spheres is no less active in restricting the imagined horizons of a genuine shift toward environmental justice. Eco-conscious millennials are routinely dismissed because they drive cars, eat food from a refrigerator, and love their cell phones. "What more do they want?" critics ask. "Try living in one of those countries without electricity," as though the only alternative to conspicuous consumption in the West is total deprivation.

Youth-led environmental activism along the lines of the Divest Harvard campaign provides powerful responses, both implicit and explicit, to the age of entitlement myth's settle-for-less logic. Audacious campaigns for entitlements to ecological health point to the fact that the choice is not between a world governed by eco-entitled young people or the absence of entitlement. There is no choosing between entitlement and no entitlement. The choice is about who deserves what, and who deserves to feel what.

Eco-policy in neoliberal society is severely limited by the foundational legal entitlement of private interests to destroy the environment to maximize profit. An economy organized around the private ownership of key productive resources reflects and reproduces the deeply rooted sense of entitlement of business classes to accumulate profits for their own advantage at the expense of everyone else and the natural environment. As Chapter 2 explains, this is the very definition of oppressive entitlement. At the start of the twenty-first century, the dominant legal framework and cultural norms disentitle young people of safe and sustainable futures.

HEALING THE METABOLIC RIFT

In the words of ecologist John Bellamy Foster (2000, 163), business as usual within the dominant framework of who is entitled to what widens "the metabolic rift" at the core of contemporary society. A rift is a crack or break in something. Picture a gap opening up in the ground after an earthquake drives apart pieces of land. When Foster talks about the metabolic rift between humans and nature opening up under capitalism, he's referring to the ways in which a profit-driven economy requires us to treat nature as though it were something totally separate from ourselves, even though humans are in fact part of nature. Certainly we are a unique part of nature; one that has the power to use nature to act on it in ways that dramatically reshapes both nature and ourselves. But being unique—both *of* nature and able to act autonomously *on* it—doesn't erase our essential "partness" of the natural environment.

An economy that is not designed to meet human–environmental needs but rather to produce private profits encourages us to erase our "partness" of nature, or at least try to forget it. Capitalist production for profit makes it "logical" to pillage the planet. Human needs for ecological sustainability become barriers to economic success. As our power to reshape the natural world develops within capitalism, which has happened dramatically since the Industrial Revolution of the 1800s, our "partness" of nature has become increasingly difficult to see. Currents of oppressive entitlement fueling for-profit economic activity sweep away our view of human needs being a piece of the needs of the planet. It can appear as though the natural environment is completely separate from human culture, a reservoir of resources for firms to draw on to produce and sell yet more commodities. The more this appears to be the case, and actually becomes the case through more aggressive forms of resource extraction, and as other environmentally harmful practices develop, the more the metabolic rift grows. The harder it is to see and act in accordance with the essential wholeness of the human/natural environment divide.

As with other harmful features of capitalism, environmental degradation is most damaging to communities already disadvantaged by economic and racial inequality. You don't find toxic waste dumps in rich neigbourhoods. They're stuck in poor, often black, working-class parts of cities, or in rural areas where Indigenous communities are left to suffer the most acute effects. Kandi Mossett (2015), an Indigenous activist in North Dakota, describes her tribe's ancestral homes as "sacrifice zones" to corporate profitability. Coal mining and fracking on the home of the Three Affiliated Tribes of the Mandan, Hidatsa, and Arikara Nations have left a trail of health and social problems. Mossett connects resource extraction in her state to cancer epidemics, a surge in traffic deaths, and a 168 percent rise in the rate of violence against women. The effects of global warming are less noticeable from Halliburton's air-conditioned Houston offices than they are in Pakistan's capital city, Karachi, where more than 1,000 people, many of them workers, died from heat exhaustion in summer 2015 (Imtiaz and ur-Rehman 2015). And as production for profit wrecks our only home and exacerbates inequality, it also abdicates our responsibility as environmental stewards. When we destroy the planet, we do it not only to ourselves but to the millions of other plant and animal species who, like us, form part of Earth's miraculous complexity.

The youth-led Idle No More movement that kicked off in late 2012 envisioned a future in which struggles for genuine democracy and ecological justice are always one and the same. On 10 January 2013, Indigenous organizers in Canada, furious with the federal government's increasingly harsh attacks on environmental protections, issued a call for "all people to join in a peaceful revolution to honour Indigenous sovereignty, and to protect the land and water" (Idle No More 2013). Since then, under the banner of Idle No More, Indigenous people in Canada, the United States, and more than a dozen other countries have been demonstrating through words and actions a radical sense of ecological entitlement. In this vision, there is no such thing as genuine rule by the people that doesn't place the needs of Earth at the core of decision making. And it is assumed that attending to ecological needs is part of governing ourselves justly.

The Assembly of Se7en Generations is a youth-education project inspired by Idle No More protests. I participated in one of its workshops at the Peoples' Social Forum held in Ottawa, Canada, in August 2014. One of the assembly's leaders, an Indigenous millennial organizer named Dianne, told me that the "seven generations" in the name of the group evokes the Great Law of traditional Haudenosaunee democracy (personal communication). That law requires that the decisions we make today take into consideration what they will mean for people seven generations from now. In Dianne's words, "everything we do today will affect the next seven generations. So we have to be conscious of how we're living [...]. If we're destroying the land, it's not going to be good for people 200 years from now."

Dianne explains that youth education in the seven generations tradition is essential to social transformation. It's part of countering the fact that politics and economic decisions in a capitalist society are driven by short-term interests in accumulating private profit:

> For us, it's about teaching our young people that the greed all over the economy today wasn't a part of our culture. There are ways of being sustainable, yet being equal—to have enough resources for everybody. I mean, this country that we

live on—this territory, this land across the nation—it has so much wealth in it, so many resources, before we even dig into the ground or anything. But we're destroying it. You know, at one point we had the freshest water in the world. And now, it's just being polluted by spills and poison. We need water to live. And so, in seven generations—that's a pretty long time away, probably about 200 years from now—how are humans going to live, if they don't have the basic water to survive? That's really scary for me to think about.

Acting in the interests of people who won't be born for more than a century involves a very different decision-making calculation than the one used in official models of Western democracy today. It also enriches our thinking about the promise and responsibility of campaigns for democratic entitlement. The framework guiding Dianne's way of being in the world views the land, the water, the animals, and the generations to come as being fully entitled to having needs met; no less deserving than humans today.

In challenging dominant political and economic practices, Idle No More organizers, students with Divest Harvard, the Standing Rock Youth opposition to the Dakota Access Pipeline (see rezpectourwater. com), and the growing number of millennial eco-activists everywhere are saying *we deserve better* than the status quo. Young activists have been at the forefront of the millions-strong marches for climate justice in the United States, Canada, Germany, France, and other places around the world. They stood on tar-soaked beaches with the "Hands Across the Sand" protests in the wake of the BP oil spill. They blockaded highways to protest Canada's "racist and paternalistic" policies during Idle No More protests dedicated to healing the metabolic rift (*CBC News* 2013). An Indigenous activist named Chelsea Vowel developed a video game called "Idle No More: Blockade" to engage more youth in the movement. In the game, you are sâkowêw, a Cree girl. Your aim is to stop the destruction of your community's Sundance field by Enkoch Industries. You halt pipeline construction "by rallying land defenders to confront the company on site" (Goldring 2014). In North Dakota, young Indigenous water protectors have put their bodies on the line to halt the construction of an oil pipeline that threatens the Missouri

River, the main source of drinking water of the Standing Rock Sioux Nation (Britto Schwartz 2016).

Like other groups at the forefront of the environmental movement, Idle No More and Divest Harvard's visions are not limited to the existing rules around who is entitled to what and who is entitled to feel what. They challenge the standard economic model that rewards the pursuit of money above all other values. They place long-term ecological justice above short-term economic gain; collective needs above the need for private profit. These groups are driven by a bold sense of entitlement and view life on Earth as entitled to new protections that would alter the very basis of society. But it is a democratic sort of entitlement, an alternative form of deservingness meant to strengthen the ability for everyone to thrive.

The challenge of building support for the social right to ecological sustainability goes far beyond listing environmental harms caused by industrial practices or more loudly trumpeting the dire situation we're in. The severity of ecological degradation is widely understood, not least by millennials, even if only in general terms. The challenge is building support for ecological entitlements based not in moralistic anti-fossil-fuelism but in alternative futures promising *better* lives, *more* opportunities, *richer* communities.

This is the core lesson I drew from South Lafourche. Within the dominant political–economic institutions, young people experience all sorts of powerful incentives not only to accept environmentally destructive ways of living but to embrace them, identify with them, defend them. Heather was sickened by what industrial production has done and threatens to do to her precious home; yet she depends on her father's job in the oil field and is proud of his skills and work ethic. In one sense, then, it's logical for millennials on the bayou to support the very systems that reproduce their own disentitlement. It's not the result of overt anti-environmentalism. It's because the only options seemingly on offer for current and future livelihoods—putting food on the table, funding community resources, developing local talent and ambition—are rooted in the oil field. And while South Lafourche is an especially illustrative example of ecological disentitlement under capitalism, the tensions that exist there run throughout all parts of the industrialized West today.

There is a strong case against a social order in which corporations are entitled to destroy the planet, the very base on which we depend to survive and thrive. It's exciting to think about a new era of democratic entitlements in which people's right to a safe and healthy environment is not just talked about but made into reality. But as Toby Rutherford of the New Orleans–based Gulf Restoration Network told me, if strengthening entitlements to ecological sustainability means casting a greener society into economic ruin, really, it's a non-starter. In Toby's advocacy for stricter regulations on the oil and gas industry in the Gulf of Mexico,

> You're talking to people who are, like, "Oil is my dad's job." Or "This is what I was planning on doing because fishing sucks now, and my only other option is to go into oil and gas." I don't have an easy answer for that. But potentially a lot of jobs are transferable. And we have a lot of infrastructure down here for technological advancement and construction. And that doesn't have to be just oil and gas. (personal communication)

The question of what uses and to what ends technology and resources will be put is a question of political will. It remains an open question—one that will be decided through struggles between social groups with contending visions of society.

One of the reasons Klein's vision of ecological sustainability as a social right is so compelling is that it doesn't root ecological sustainability in a politics of sacrifice. To be sure, an ecologically just future won't include zillionaires zipping around on private jets to mansions on every continent. But these sorts of sacrifices touch such a small, self-isolated segment of the population that they're virtually irrelevant to democratic debates over different visions of ecological and economic justice. Klein emphasizes that for most people, an ecologically sustainable future will mean *better* lives, not deprivation: healthier job sites; less time commuting; the expansion of public services such as health care, education, transit; more affordable housing. In other words, Klein's vision takes the problem of South Lafourche seriously. Recognizing that existing economic structures severely limit the options available to many people, she doesn't moralize about individual life choices. Nor does she expect catastrophic pronouncements about the state of things to shock people into eco-action. She argues that people will begin to turn away from business as usual when ecologically and economically just alternatives become genuine options; and in the Northern Cheyenne Reservation and other experiments like it, there's proof that Klein is right.

STFU, CLIMATE CHANGE APOLOGISTS

January to April 2015 was the hottest January to April of any year on record. It formed part of the hottest 12-month period on record since the previous April (Romm 2015). That same sizzling April, an article appeared in the *New York Post* headlined "STFU Millennials" (Dawson 2015). In case you don't know the acronym, U stands for "up," and ST stands for "shut the." In this piece, parenting columnist Mackenzie Dawson regurgitates the familiar accusation that millennials have "helped themselves to an extra portion at the entitlement buffet." Because her thinking is restricted within the dominant age of entitlement narrative, Dawson's commentary isn't concerned with actual challenges confronting young people, least of all challenges posed by the threat of ecological collapse. She conceives of the millennial crisis in terms of young people expecting everything to be handed to them without having to work for it. Accordingly, she counsels millennials to say please and thank you in emails and to pay more respect to people who have more experience than they do. She has nothing to say about the environment.

Read in the context of the millennial environmental crisis, Dawson's tsk-tsking is like wringing hands over the paint job on the house consumed by flames. If it were just that her type of argument misses the point it wouldn't be so distressing. The problem is that the myth of the age of entitlement counteracts the work of young people who are attempting to make good on the idea that everyone deserves to live in a society genuinely committed to ecological sustainability. The age of entitlement myth underwrites a vision of society in which the fundamental decisions about how we live together on the planet are determined not by the needs of humans and all living things, but by the quest to drive up private profits. This poses an extreme threat not only to the future of humanity, but to all life on Earth.

In spite of the harm climate change is already causing and grave warnings about the destruction to come, the future of the Earth and our relationship to it remains an open question. Ecological health, which includes human wellness, depends on struggles. On one side, there are movements pressing for a twenty-first century extension of democratic entitlements to include the actual guarantee of a healthy, safe, sustainable environment for everyone. On the other side are corporate and state interests favoring the continuation of systems that legitimize oppressive entitlements protecting the rights of a small portion of society to enrich itself through the destruction of land, water, air, and life forms of all kinds. Choosing a side, whether actively or by inaction, will be one of the most important decisions you'll ever make.

CHAPTER SIX

EVERYTHING FOR EVERYBODY

FEELIN' THE BERN

Emerging from the subway in New York City's Bronx borough, I heard the unmistakable sound of a large crowd cheering. Not yet two weeks into spring 2016, I was still carrying my windbreaker after 6:00 p.m. Along with the stream of people entering St. Mary's Park, I climbed a stone staircase between tennis courts and monkey bars, our path guided by blue police tape. The tape divided the core of the rally in the park's bowl from the overflow section on an adjacent baseball diamond. To my left, a man wearing a Yankees' cap said he'd heard the park already held 5,000 people. The *New York Times* later reported that the number of rally-goers swelled to 18,500.

I stood on a hill that formed one side of the park's grassy bowl. The crowd below chanted a single word, stressing each of its two syllables: "Ber-nie! Ber-nie! Ber-nie!" Vermont Senator Bernie Sanders's campaign for "a political revolution" had arrived in New York City.

Weeks earlier, a CNN pundit called Sanders's campaign to become the Democratic Party's 2016 presidential candidate "this year's biggest story." Sally Kohn (2016) wrote that "Sanders has already changed the election with his dogged focus on income inequality and economic justice." She drew closer to the main significance of Sanders's success when writing that his supporters "will change elections and politics for decades to come." Bernie himself was 74 at the time of his run to head the Democratic Party. His campaign was led by legions of newly politicized millennials demanding extensive new social rights and deeper democracy.

Sanders's support from millennial voters towered over that of the other leading candidates. He regularly won more than 80 percent of the votes cast by people between the ages of 18 and 29 (Kohn 2016). Looking back on the primaries, a *Washington Post* article was headlined "More Young People Voted for Bernie Sanders than Trump and Clinton Combined—By a Lot" (Blake 2016). In St. Mary's Park, I sensed the historic importance of this millennial political awakening. I passed a college student wearing a rainbow-sleeved T-shirt and holding a blue, red, and yellow sign that read "Bronx Is Feelin' the Bern!" Not far from her a group of teens strapped in backpacks laughed while taking turns trying on a Bernie-style unkempt wig. "Bernie!" buttons were pinned to jean jackets, leather jackets, hoodies, and baseball jerseys. They showed a cartoon version of Sanders's easily recognizable silhouette. In this crowd, thick glasses and two tufts of unruly hair could only belong to one man. Buttons declared "Education Is a Right!"

Sanders first addressed the crowd in the overflow section. He stood on a makeshift platform made of an overturned audio equipment carrying case. Thousands of outstretched hands holding cell phones pointed at Sanders as he stepped up to the platform and shouted "It looks like the South Bronx is ready for a political revolution!" Sanders's thick Brooklyn accent disappeared under cheers of delight. Cell phones joggled overhead. Sanders repeated the sentence; then more cheering, more jumping, more chants of "Bernie!" erupting all around. Sanders listed the key policy planks in his campaign to be president: free college tuition; publicly funded health care accessible to all; a minimum wage hike to $15 per hour; more government funding to help create jobs, build infrastructure, and address health problems caused by environmental degradation, problems that are especially severe in poor and racialized communities like the Bronx. At the end of each sentence, he was interrupted by cheering.

Sanders referred to this policy vision as "democratic socialism" (Murphy 2015). He argued that a socialist system would improve the living standards of most of people. Currently, the wealth produced across society is disproportionately captured by a small group of individuals and corporations at the top of the socioeconomic ladder. Wealth should be shared more equitably throughout society. In recent decades, most political commentators in the United States, including many self-identified socialists, assumed that the word *socialism* would be radioactive to any serious contender for electoral office. When Kshama Sawant was elected to Seattle's city council in 2013, she was the first person to run as a socialist to do so since 1877. Are political possibilities changing? A poll in February 2016 showed that millennials favored socialism over capitalism as "the most compassionate system" by 58 to 33 percent (Walsh 2016). Writer Anis Shivani (2016) argues that "millennials, compared to previous generations, are exceptionally receptive to socialism." In his words, economic and social problems that millennials did not choose

> have forced them to think outside the capitalist paradigm, which reduces human beings to figures of sales and productivity, and to consider if in their immediate lives, and in the organization of larger collectivities, there might not be more cooperative, nonviolent, mutually beneficial arrangements with better measures of human happiness than GDP growth or other statistics that benefit the financial class.

As Bernie was shepherded to the rally's main stage, the overflow crowd crossed the baseball diamond to watch his speech on a large screen. Zlata, a 23-year-old white woman from Brooklyn, shook her head and smiled: "The energy of the crowd is so amazing!" (personal communication). She stood next to an old friend she'd arrived with and a new friend met at the rally. Zlata said that before witnessing the surging support for Sanders's campaign, "it felt like whatever you do … it won't make a difference." She acknowledged that millennials get criticized for being "lazy or complacent." But she argued that we need to understand the broader social context to get why people choose to be politically active or not. "During the Vietnam War," she reasoned, "when people were advocating and revolting against that, they were so passionate because they thought they could make a difference. Maybe since then we've seen that it doesn't make a difference; so why even try? That's why I wasn't into politics until now. You know?" Ted, the new friend, jumped in: "We have something to rally behind now."

Ted is a freelance information technology worker. The black hat he wore at the rally was adorned with an image of the first Nintendo controller, which was released in 1985, four years before Ted was born. He started college but didn't graduate. He worries that without a degree he may never find a secure, well-paying job. He said that being a black man makes his shot at a good job that much harder. Like Zlata, he says millennials are drawn to the Sanders campaign "because we want to be moved by something. We don't want to keep repeating the same old problems of our parents. We want a revolution. We want to break away from that status quo."

The two bounced ideas back and forth about why millennials are attracted to Sanders's message:

ZLATA: Bernie's been saying all the things that ...
TED: ... that you've been thinking ...
ZLATA: ... yeah, that our *class* has been thinking, that minorities have been thinking ...
TED: Absolutely.
ZLATA: And now ... we have a voice. And that's the most important thing.
TED: We're here ... we're fighting for it.

Opponents of the Sanders campaign said *get real*. An editorialist for the *Washington Post* wrote that Sanders's campaign "is not about governing in the real world of trade-off and constraints. Which is to say, it is not about governing at all" (Stromberg 2016). With all the subtlety of a boot to the head, the Republican candidate for president, Donald Trump, called Sanders "a maniac" (in Griswold 2015). Speaking at a Republican rally, Trump said, "this socialist-slash-communist, okay? Nobody wants to say it. [...] He's gonna tax you people at 90 percent; he's gonna take everything." Republican pollster Frank Luntz said the rising popularity of socialism among youth "should frighten you. Because if it's cool today, it's going to change American politics tomorrow" (Durkin 2016). Op-eds with titles like "Bernie Sanders Needs to Get Serious on Foreign Policy" appeared routinely in major newspapers (Ignatius 2016).

And it wasn't only self-identified conservatives who attacked Sanders's socialist policy vision. Many Democrats and others who call themselves liberals or "on the Left" dismissed the Sanders vision for being unserious, unrealistic. The left-leaning political columnist Jonathan Chait (2016) called the Sanders campaign a "political fantasy" that relies on "magical-realism" instead of practical policy plans. Hillary Clinton, who beat Sanders in the race to become the Democratic Party's presidential candidate, suggested his plans for publicly funded college and universal health care were "pie in the sky stuff" (in Merica 2016). She repeatedly referred to herself as "a progressive who likes to get things done" (in Covert 2016), implying that Sanders's ideas, even if appealing, aren't realistic enough to expect to be implemented.

The vision of society that drew millions of people to Sanders were his promises of "guaranteed economic rights for all Americans" (in Murphy 2015). It praised countries that have implemented robust redistributive policies "protecting the needs of their working families, the elderly, the children, the sick, and the poor." It stood in solidarity with "African Americans who are right to proclaim the moral principle that Black Lives Matter." And it promised immigration reform "that gives Hispanics and others a pathway to citizenship and a better life." Legions of millennial Sandernistas urged their fellow citizens to raise their expectations of being entitled to social rights and stronger democratic control over the economy. The Bernie moment demonstrated that there is mass millennial appetite for a new era of expanded democratic entitlements.

Opposition to Sanders and his supporters echoed the myth of the age of entitlement. Friendly and hostile critics alike spoke with a unified voice: Lower your expectations. House of Representative member John Lewis, a supporter of Hillary Clinton, said Sanders's promise of expanded social rights is "the wrong message to send to any group. There's not anything free in America. We all have to pay for something. Education is not free. Health care is not free. Food is not free. Water is not free. I think it's very misleading to say to the American people, we're going to give you something free" (in Atlanta Journal-Constitution 2016). Remember the quote in the opening chapter from a speech by Kevin Spacey's *House of Cards* character President Frank Underwood? He might have been channeling John Lewis: "You are entitled to nothing."

The Sanders campaign helped reopen debates about what social supports everyone deserves and what responsibilities we must assume for taking care of each other. Debates about where to draw the line between reasonable and excessive entitlements reflect different visions of society. Listening to Zlata talk about how much richer, happier, and healthier we all could be in a society devoted not to maximizing corporate profits but to meeting human needs, I was reminded of a slogan chanted by workers and students in demonstrations in Italy in the 1970s: "Allt åt Alla!" (Everything for everybody!) (Katsiaficas 2006). What if instead of the assumption that "there's not anything free" in this world, our societies were organized on the commitment to ensuring "everything for everybody"? New York University Professor Kristin Ross (2015, 1) wrote a book about the efforts of Parisians in 1871 to establish a world of "communal luxury" through a mass uprising. For more than two months the democratic insurgency "transformed the city of Paris into an autonomous Commune and set about improvising the free organization of its social life according to principles of association and cooperation." The history of democratic social movements is an archive that proves another world is possible.

However, Bernie Sanders's campaign for social rights was not the only appeal to people disaffected by politics as usual in the 2016 presidential election. The Republican Party's nominee, Donald Trump, promised to "Make America Great Again" (Trump 2016). The slogan is hopeful and demonstrated widespread appeal. Trump became president after winning more Electoral College votes (though not more votes in total) than Hillary Clinton. Trump's campaign rhetoric conjured images of a better future. It invited people to feel entitled to greatness and to work toward recovering lost glory. But the Trump campaign was very clear about its intention to ensure greatness to some by denying it to others.

Trump associated a return to greatness with an anti-immigrant, racist, pro-business policy framework. The *New York Times* wrote that Trump has "opened the door to assertions of white identity and resentment in a way not seen so broadly in American culture in over half a century" (Confessore 2016). He promised to build "the greatest wall you have ever seen" along the US–Mexico border (Martosko 2015). He said it would protect hardworking Americans from foreign criminals and people looking for a handout. "And just to finish," Trump was fond of saying, "you know who's going to pay for the wall? Mexico. With all the money that they have taken from us." A Trump presidency, the man promised, would deport 11 million undocumented people living in the United States. It would ban Muslims from entering the country. He was frequently openly sexist in speeches and interviews. He bragged about sexually assaulting women.

In Trump's campaign vision, certain people in the United States were ensured that greatness was on the horizon. Others were told that they deserved nothing and would be forced to leave the country. Access to greatness—being entitled to be great again—depended on where you were born, the color of your skin, your gender, your religion, and the size of your bank account. If you were white, an American-born citizen, a Christian, a rich banker, a macho true patriot you were entitled to be great again, and good times were coming. If you were Muslim, an undocumented worker, on welfare, a feminist, or a critic of Trump's you were entitled to nothing. The greatness promised to some depended on the deprivation of others.

Both the Sanders and Trump campaigns were built on the idea that the real entitlement framework is currently unbalanced and needs to be reset. Sanders promised to do so through nourishing currents of democratic entitlement. Trump embodied and encouraged his followers to cultivate currents of oppressive entitlement. Recalling the framework laid out in Chapter 2, institutions, ideas, feelings, and actions that protect or aim to extend collective forms of deservingness and self-government in all areas of life are democratic forms of entitlement. Those that protect or deepen the privilege of certain individuals or groups through the subordination of others in relation to existing forms of social inequality are oppressive forms of entitlement.

We'll never know what American voters would've chosen had the choice been between the Sanders version and the Trump version of change. The Democratic Party chose Hillary Clinton, who campaigned on a platform of policy as usual. Clinton's candidacy offered the possibility of electing the first woman president, but at the same time, in light of her track record as President Obama's secretary of state, senator for New York, and core advisor in Bill Clinton's White House, she personified 30 years of neoliberal governance. There is evidence that voters would've chosen Sanders over Trump (deBoer 2016). As it was, in the contest between Clinton's defense of the status quo and Trump's promise of radical change, Trump won.

We appear to be at a crucial historical juncture in choosing and building a vision of the future. The same anti-immigrant, racist, exclusionary politics that fueled the Trump campaign was the driving force behind the "Leave" side in the 2016 referendum that saw the United Kingdom quit the European Union (Seymour 2016). It is possible that, as the remaining threads of universal entitlement to having needs met are shredded, and as the people and organizations that helped bring them into being pass away, there will be a historic lowering and hardening of expectations even beyond what's already happened. As social rights are destroyed and social exclusion intensifies, fear and anger will become more widespread. Where those feelings are channeled will depend on what political options are available. In the absence of mass mobilization against pro-inequality Trump-like visions of society, currents of oppressive entitlement will likely consolidate inequality where it currently exists and create new layers of social hierarchy.

A different possibility is that movements for democratic entitlement develop, spread, and grow to the point that they halt the intensification of inequality that's taken place during the neoliberal era and begin to reverse the trend by establishing institutions and making policies that not only combat economic and social inequality, but also aim to meet human and ecological needs. Recent years have seen modest victories in this direction: winning a $15 minimum wage in certain US jurisdictions; halting tuition increases in Quebec; forcing certain universities to adopt more ecologically sustainable investment policies. The real entitlement framework is never fixed for all time. There's a chance it could be rebalanced toward democracy and equality.

We can make arguments about how things ought to be; we can develop reasonable predictions based on rigorous observations of the present balance of forces in society. But there is no way of abstractly working out who will be entitled to what resources and who will be entitled to feel what in advance of the struggles that shape what is normal from one historical period to the next. Individuals and groups possess agency. People have the capacity to act on the world to change it for the better. Questions about what the real entitlement framework of the future will look like will be answered through social struggles. It's in the context of these struggles over the future that we need to understand the power of the myth of the age of entitlement and the importance of rejecting it.

ENVISIONING LESS

The myth of the age of entitlement involves both a description of current social trends and a vision of how society ought to be. In this narrative, Generation Y is more excessively and more harmfully entitled than any previous generation. Millennials are said to hold unrealistically high expectations about what resources they deserve access to and what emotions they deserve to feel.

Description is paired with a value judgment. Those who describe millennial entitlement tend to do so to condemn it. We are warned that entitled students are not only diminishing the quality of higher education, but they are developing habits that will turn them into entitled workers. Entitled workers are portrayed as obstacles to economic productivity. A "nation of takers" is an unhappy community, says demographer Nicholas Eberstadt (2012) in a book subtitled *America's Entitlement Epidemic*. This threatens society's fundamental values and institutions.

The value judgment leads to a demand: Millennials, and those who come after them, must expect less. Peddlers of the age of entitlement myth rarely sketch a detailed plan for a better world. Yet the essence of their vision of the most desirable future is not difficult to see. The age of entitlement storyline is an argument for young people to lower their expectations of having needs met outside markets. It reflects a

vision of society opposed to social rights and genuine collective decision making. It conceives of the ideal citizen as a savvy consumer who
is fully self-reliant for his or her own individual survival. It assumes
that racism, sexism, and other forms of discrimination can be resolved
by individuals acting kinder within the existing social order.

Psychologist Jean Twenge (in Quenqua 2013, Twenge and Campbell
2009) offers the most widely promoted solution to the problem of what
she calls "the narcissism epidemic": Millennials should be more grateful
for what they have. The president of the American Enterprise Institute
declares "Choosing to focus on good things makes you feel better than
focusing on bad things" (A. Brooks 2015). *New York Times* columnist
David Brooks (2015) encourages everyone to develop "dispositional
gratitude" in order for people to appreciate that "they are given far
more than they pay for—and are much richer than they deserve."

Business analysts say millennial employees should be thankful to
have any job at all. Young people who work hard will advance; taking
their licks builds character. Education reformers say millennial students shouldn't expect government handouts to support their education. If they want a degree, they should expect to pay for it; learning
to manage their finances better will be good for them. Perhaps they'll
get serious and learn something that business leaders need and stop
with the liberal arts and other flights of fancy that Gen Y appears to
expect university to be about. State and corporate officials say millennial protestors are "overreacting, hysterical, entitled and coddled"
(McClennen 2015). Young people need to get real both about how
politics and the economy works and the limits to what policy changes
are possible. Millennials need to expect less.

MISREPRESENTING THE TRUTH

The age of entitlement storyline has it wrong. Generation Y is not
floating languidly on a sea of modern riches; nor can Gen Y as a
group be said to hold unprecedentedly high expectations about what
it deserves. In fact, drops in key quality of life measures show that
millennials are entitled to comparatively less than what was taken for
granted by their parents' generations.

As discussed in Chapter 3, the proportion of young people who will end up with a good working-class job is smaller today than it was in the 1960s, and it continues to shrink. The new normal in the work world includes short-term contracts, part-time hours, low pay, no benefits, no pension, and no union protections. The precariousness of workers left out of the expansion in welfare state entitlements has become the new normal across the working class.

Chapter 4 showed that while millennials are entering postsecondary institutions in record numbers, college costs more than ever and public funding for education has been cut. Student debt has reached pandemic levels. Millennials who are prevented from attending college face even steeper challenges as adults. Major trends in postsecondary teaching—ballooning class sizes, the replacement of face-to-face learning with online instruction, and the promotion of entrepreneurialism as the essential ethic of our time—provide Generation Y with a less-human college experience than the best models developed during earlier moments in the age of mass higher education.

Chapter 5 showed that the threat of ecological collapse is more severe and more pressing for millennials than for any previous generation. Some millennials are active in movements for ecological justice. But contrary to the myth of the age of entitlement, many young people are resigned to the likelihood that their world will be one of chronic environmental degradation and the attendant harmful consequences for the reproduction of our species and all life on Earth.

Specific changes in the workplace, on campuses, and in the natural environment are happening against the backdrop of a shrinking social safety net. Compared to the high point of the welfare state period before the millennial era, unemployment insurance is harder to access today and provides relatively less support. Citizens have to wait longer before receiving old-age pensions. Budgets for food stamps and other welfare programs have been cut. Young people—especially young people of color—are more likely to be incarcerated. Disentitlement is core to the millennial condition.

The age of entitlement myth wrongly collapses distinct forms of deservingness into a universally negative category. It is likely that, left unchallenged, the myth has a narrowing effect on political debate. Its description of the problem of millennial entitlement comes with a built-in solution: Young people need to expect less. The myth creates special challenges for young people already dispossessed by everyday racism, sexism, homophobia, economic inequality, and other forms of discrimination. It is anti-democratic to use the concept of entitlement to condemn all claims of deserving better than what already exists.

Cultural theorist Sara Ahmed (2014b) makes a similar point about the power of the concept of "willfulness" to shut down marginalized voices. Being described as "willful," writes Ahmed, is to be accused of being "too assertive, even pushy" (20). Yet being accused of being "willful" is more likely to happen to some groups than others. The word *willful* is applied to children, "feminist killjoys," and others in positions of subordination who willfully seek to satisfy their desires (2–3). It is not applied to other groups who certainly exercise strong wills in having their desires met, but whose desires being met is part of business as usual (e.g., rich people, white men, and tenured university professors). Being accused of being willful occurs unevenly and has uneven consequences. Similarly, being accused of being entitled, being pressed to accept less social support, might not be a problem for the relatively small layer of the millennial generation born into riches and lofty social status. However, for working-class people, immigrants, women, and others who face discrimination, being accused of being entitled, being pressed to settle for less, is a grave threat to well-being. The age of entitlement narrative needs to be rejected because it undercuts the life chances and living standards of all but the privileged and wealthy. It ignores complex inclusions and exclusions running along lines of race, class, and gender.

THE PROBLEM WITH COMMON SENSE

But if millennials are being forced to survive with less, why do we think they demand so much? Why has the myth of the age of entitlement become part of our collective common sense at precisely the moment when millions of young people are facing disentitlement on the job, at school, and in their communities?

Understanding the prominence of the myth requires examining the socioeconomic context in which it was born and rose to dominance.

The idea that, compared to previous generations, millennials expect more for doing less did not develop in a vacuum. Ideas never do. It might be useful to look at changes in parenting techniques, technology, and consumer culture to understand the millennial condition; but clearly identifying the role of such things is possible only if we're also keenly sensitive to how changes in our whole socioeconomic order have shaped our own vantage point on what's a reasonable or excessive sense of entitlement. The language and symbols and interpretive frameworks we use to make sense of the world develop in relation to the material conditions that shape how we live.

The dominant socioeconomic trends in more than 40 years of neoliberalism include the privatization of public goods, responsibility for survival being downloaded onto individuals, the normalization of precariousness for growing sections of the working class, and growing economic inequality. The generation condemned for being more entitled than any in history graduated high school during the all-but-total evisceration of the postwar welfare state economic model. Millennials were moving by the millions into the full-time labor force at precisely the moment that the bottom fell out of the economy in 2008–09.

During a crisis of capitalist profitability, as employers are laying off workers and warning that they may need to close shop, expressions of deservingness on the part of working people (deserving better pay, deserving time off, deserving to hold onto benefits) are more easily framed as being unreasonable. Since the crisis, business and state policymakers have spoken with a single voice: People are going to have to learn to do with less. In a period when the official view sees it as necessary and normal for people to lower their expectations, anybody who expects something better is more easily portrayed as unjustifiably entitled.

The organizations and cultural resources that were once the best defenders and promoters of democratic entitlement have been weakened or destroyed by 40 years of neoliberalism. When the boundaries of mainstream political debate aren't pressed open by a robust Left alternative, explanations that favor privileged social groups, like the age of entitlement storyline or Donald Trump's campaign to strengthen oppressive entitlements, can appear to be the only way of making sense of things. There are material consequences to the lack of widely accessible alternative visions of social and environmental justice.

Alan Sears (2014, 4) uses the term "infrastructures of dissent" to talk about the web of formal and informal groups and networks that challenge exploitation and oppression at work, at school, and in communities, both locally and globally. Throughout most of the twentieth century, infrastructures of dissent were much stronger and more influential in mainstream politics than they are today. Powerful labor unions, social democratic parties, robust radical organizations on campuses, and anti-capitalist currents in popular culture played significant roles in shaping public debate and policy. They promoted and defended democratic entitlements such as union rights and worker protections, citizenship benefits, full civil rights for all, reproductive rights, and other specific material entitlements guaranteed by the state. They helped build up and sustain mass senses of entitlement to having needs met. They provided alternative frameworks for understanding socioeconomic struggles.

The disappearance of twentieth-century infrastructures of dissent has left workers, poor people, and marginalized groups more vulnerable to having democratic entitlements rolled back. For example, in jurisdictions where the rate of union membership has declined, living standards have also gone down—not just for union members, but for everyone (Freeman et al. 2015). In the absence of large campus coalitions for social justice, college programs that challenge the entrepreneurial thrust of Austerity U are frequently targeted for budget cuts. In periods without robust infrastructures of dissent, frustration with business as usual often takes the form of private anger, sadness, disaffection, and resignation to the harsh reality of this moment.

The Pulitzer Prize–winning author Chris Hedges (2015, 5) argues that people tend to become unruly when there is a growing "gap between what people want, and indeed expect, and what they get." Certainly there have been periods in history when the gap between high expectations and falling living standards has led to revolutionary movements for greater democracy and equality. But periods of declining living standards can also drive down what people feel is reasonable to expect.

I was particularly struck by declining common sense feelings of entitlement during a conversation at the SHOREline Summit (discussed in Chapter 5). The SHOREline team from Thibodaux High School was represented in New Orleans by three women of color. Their exhibition table in the ballroom was backed by yellow cardboard with the words "Monarch Joint Venture" spelled out in multicolored letters. Their project, "Our Happy Place," was designed to "increase community disaster preparedness and recovery efforts by increasing community resiliency" through the beautification of an underused city park. The park, freshened up by community artwork, a butterfly garden, and new play structures made from old tires, was meant to serve not only as a community meeting place in the event of a natural disaster but as an incubator for "a sense of togetherness" in tranquil times. During Thibodaux's presentation, Lateesha thanked a hardware store for donating paint to their project. The paint, which couldn't be sold because its expiry date had passed, was on its way to being thrown out when it was diverted to the SHOREline chapter. The same year it donated paint to "Our Happy Place," this hardware store chain made more than $50 billion in sales.

I knelt beside the butterfly net and asked the three teens whether they wished the hardware store had donated more to their project. All three answered "no" in unison, and each again expressed gratitude for the expired paint (personal communication). I pressed the issue. "But you thought it was OK to ask for the paint; and the store thought it was OK to give it to you," I needled. "This corporation has billions of dollars. Shouldn't it have chipped in more to improve the quality of your community contribution?" Again, my suggestion was flatly rebuffed by the whole group. Lateesha said we "can't live off handouts." Charmaine explained the hardware store "ain't always gonna be there to lean on." Cindy added it would be a mistake even to expect the store to continue donating expired paint. The more intensely I argued they should feel entitled to more help, the more intensely they argued against feeling entitled to anything. "We work for everything we have," said Lateesha—"and that's how it should be." Charmaine added, with a tone suggesting she wasn't interested in an answer: "If you don't work, how you gonna learn?"

As the vision of society based in the rule of the market becomes more firmly established, people's sense of what is normal to expect outside of market transactions is narrowed. Social rights can appear unrealistic when it is increasingly rare to have needs satisfied other than through consumer activity. The routine experience of having expectations go unmet can lead people to lower their expectations. Resigning yourself to narrow hopes is precisely what the age of entitlement narrative counsels in clashes between millennial expectations of the good life and state and business policy in the age of neoliberal austerity. If infrastructures of dissent were more vibrant, there's a good chance that SHOREliners in Thibodaux wouldn't feel so undeserving of a bit more free paint. Perhaps Trump's campaign to fix contemporary problems by radically strengthening oppressive entitlements wouldn't have attracted so much support if people had the chance to choose an alternative campaign for radical democratic entitlements.

RESETTING THE REAL ENTITLEMENT FRAMEWORK

Yes, the millennial era is beset by a terrible problem of entitlement. But it's not the one we've heard so much about in the age of entitlement myth. The real problem lies in the institutions, actions, and ideas that embed hierarchy into the core of society, making vastly unequal and harmful systems of entitlement appear to be neutral, normal aspects of the social order. There is no such thing as a society without entitlement. Every society is organized around rules and practices establishing the line between deserving and undeserving. *All societies have a real entitlement framework.* It consists of formal and informal institutions and values establishing who is entitled to access what resources and who is entitled to feel what. You may prefer one or another entitlement framework: This one is just and good; that one is unfair and must be scrapped. But you cannot be against the general concept of deservingness.

In the years since the 2008 economic crash, at the same time as improvements in most working people's lives were "weak" or "underwhelming" or "sluggish" or "nonexistent," the small group of wealthy shareholders and owners at the top of the socioeconomic ladder saw unprecedented economic gains. As a headline in the *Wall Street Journal* noted: "Some 95% of 2009–2012 Income Gains Went to Wealthiest 1%" (Cronin 2013). Between 2009 and 2015, the wealth of the richest

1,000 families in the United Kingdom grew by 112 percent (Garside 2015). This made these 1,000 families worth more than the poorest 40 percent of UK households combined. In the decade following the Great Recession, stock prices and corporate profits reached historic highs, even as there were fewer Americans working than before the 2008 crash. A *New York Times* article sums up the trend: "Corporate profits are at their highest level in at least 85 years. Employee compensation is at the lowest level in 65 years" (Norris 2014).

Yet as Derek Thompson (2013) noted in *The Atlantic*, when we zoom the lens back to view the years since the crash in broader historical context we see that "this isn't a 'recession' trend. It's just a trend that the recession has amplified." Corporate profits began pulling away from wages in the 1970s, surging ahead in the 1990s, and exploding since the 2000s. How do we explain this yawning wealth gap? The answer comes down to a powerful movement for the limitless entitlement of business and political elites. Tax, trade, and labor policies supported by anti-democratic ideas like the so-called problem of runaway millennial entitlement have effectively entitled those at the top to more of the pie than ever. Neoliberalism is best understood as a massive transfer of wealth from those at the bottom—waged and unwaged workers, immigrants, poor people, Indigenous peoples—to wealthy individuals and corporations at the top. And those at the top feel entitled to their privileges; so entitled, in fact, that they've managed to keep most of us from seeing concentrated wealth as an oppressive entitlement.

One unintended consequence of the myth of the age of entitlement is that it invites questions about whether millennials might actually deserve *better* than the status quo. The argument that Generation Y has unreasonably high expectations opens up space for a counterargument. The most powerful counterarguments are made not in books but through struggles for democratic entitlement throughout society. Broad-based, coordinated campaigns for social justice can clarify real political and economic inequalities, shining light on how the entitlement of some groups depends on the disentitlement of others. Millennials have been at the forefront of many of these struggles. From Occupy Wall Street to Black Lives Matter to the Fight for $15 to the Quebec student strike to pipeline resistance and other movements for ecological justice to the Bernie Sanders moment ... the past decade has seen periodic surges of mass mobilization for democratic entitlement in all sorts of different contexts. Polls suggest that today's college students are "more politically engaged than they have been in decades" (Zinshteyn 2016). The challenge is to build infrastructures of dissent for the twenty-first century that will help turn bursts of anger and hope into durable, powerful movements for social rights and deeper democracy.

Working in counterflow to dominant institutions and ideas is, by definition, a struggle. Expanding democratic entitlements will be especially challenging under a Trump administration. Yet the future of democracy, equality, and environmental health depends on struggles for social and ecological justice—for expanding human and environmental entitlements to have needs and desires met. The most powerful struggles will spark new moments of mass insurgency like those that marked the high days of Black Lives Matter and the Quebec student strike. No less important will be establishing the organizations and communication networks that allow us to learn from these moments—both their victories and their shortcomings—and transform our learning into stronger movements in the future. Millennials have been unfairly cast as holding excessive expectations. It's in the interests of everyone and the planet itself that young people begin to expect much more, creating new visions and new systems for providing everything for everybody.

APPENDIX

A NOTE ON METHODOLOGY

"What Does a Millennial Look Like?" This headline tops an April 2016 article on *The Awl* (Ihaza 2016). It stands above a photograph of two white men. Both are holding cell phones. One man appears to be taking a selfie of the two of them. The background is out of focus, but it looks as though they're in an urban area, possibly under a highway overpass. Both men are wearing well-groomed beards, black leather jackets, sunglasses, and hair styled with a product that makes it look shiny. Neither man is smiling into the camera; in fact, one shows a hint of a sneer. Jeff Ihaza writes that we're looking at the version of the millennial "that has come to dominate our consciousness: middle-class, educated, white kids."

More millennials do not graduate college than do. On average, the standard of living millennials can expect will be lower than that of their parents' generation. More millennials live in nonurban areas than in cities. And Gen Y is the most ethnically diverse generation in the history of the United States. Ihaza argues that a lot is left out by the familiar assumption that the millennial "is a white bespectacled young man you find in Williamsburg" or any other urban neighborhood of hipster cool.

The stereotypical millennial Ihaza describes is the focus of the myth of the age of entitlement. Because my book focuses on that myth, I'm very interested in popular portrayals of millennials. However, I'm no less interested in the actual experiences of millennials that get left out of common sense ideas about Generation Y. My inquiry into what's included in, and what's excluded from, popular depictions of millennials has been informed by three types of research.

First, I've tracked representations of millennials in news media, scholarly research, and popular culture. For example, I used Google Alerts to stay up to date on news stories about "the age of entitlement" and "Generation Y." I followed academic research on millennials by conducting keyword searches in scholarly journal databases. I frequently searched for stories about the millennial condition in independent media, such as *Democracy Now*, *AlterNet*, and *Counterpunch*. I watched countless films, television shows, and YouTube clips spoofing or attempting to portray millennial experiences realistically.

My book cites more nonacademic sources (news articles, opinion pieces, television shows) than you might expect in a social science text written for university students. However, the book's main contribution is an alternative perspective on a contemporary debate playing out in popular culture. I've drawn extensively on popular sources in an attempt to bring the debate to life in the language and tone we experience in our everyday lives.

Second, I've conducted interviews with more than 50 millennials in different parts of Canada and the United States (primarily in the Greater Toronto Area, New York City, and southern Louisiana). I also interviewed more than 20 journalists, academics, and activists of various ages. The interviews with young people attempted to learn more about millennial experiences that get left out of the age of entitlement myth. I wanted to hear young activists, precarious workers, people of color, and others who don't neatly fit the stereotype of a millennial talk in their own words about their daily routines, hopes, and fears. For example, we know that "the average 29-year-old" in America does not live in an urban area; yet rurality is not associated with millennialness (Thompson 2016). I deliberately conducted interviews with millennials in rural Louisiana (see Chapter 5) in hopes of shedding fuller light on the experiences of Gen Y's nonurban cohort.

It was never my intention to gather a statistically representative sample or use interviews to make conclusive generalizations. The interviews sought descriptions that are unique to conversations, to enrich our understanding of what statistics suggest about underrepresented millennial experiences. Interview subjects whose work places them in the public eye—journalists and scholars, for example—are identified by their real names. The rest of my interview subjects were promised anonymity, so they are referred to by pseudonyms. All interviews are cited in-text only as "personal communication"; they do not appear in the References.

Third, I've used formal social theory to make sense of and comment on patterns emerging from my textual and interview research. My approach has been guided by work in the tradition of Antonio Gramsci, an Italian activist and theorist writing in the 1920s and 1930s. Gramsci witnessed the rise of fascism in Italy. He spent years in a fascist prison after being arrested for campaigning for democracy and socialism. Stunned by the sudden popular embrace of fascism, Gramsci was especially concerned about how certain ideas achieve the status of common sense. He used the term *common sense* as shorthand for widely taken-for-granted assumptions throughout society about what is real, what is desirable, and what is possible to change. In the notes Gramsci (1971) wrote while in prison, he developed powerful insights into how common sense ideas are formed, contested, and transformed. He argued that the process involves much more than rational debate, symbolic persuasion, or any other tactic that occurs exclusively at the level of language.

Gramsci's great insight, which is a theoretical lodestar in my analysis of the myth of the age of entitlement, is that common sense is formed in relation to the material conditions structuring our lives at work, school, and in our communities. As Alan Sears (2003, 6) writes, although common sense ideas "take on a fact-like solidity," they are often shot through with contradictions, and they are always capable of changing in accordance with changes in socioeconomic struggles. Struggles over who has access to what goods and services and who is entitled to make political and economic decisions are both informed by common sense and have the power to shift what ideas achieve the status of common sense in the future. I use Gramsci's framework to better understand the struggles that produced the myth of the age of entitlement, as well as the efforts by millennial-led social movements to forge new ways of organizing society, which, in turn, will cultivate new forms of common sense.

Finally, it's worth saying something about how my own experiences as a millennial-ish university professor inform my approach to these issues. My relationship with the millennial generation is, in the terminology of Facebook, "complicated." According to the sociologists Howe and Strauss (2000), who assert that the first millennials were born in 1982, my being born in 1979 means that I don't qualify as a millennial. I'm not a Gen-Xer either, though, if you assume they stopped being born in the mid-1970s, which most people who place weight in these categories do. I came of age during the height of the millennial era, and millennials have been among my closest friends all my life. My cultural tastes have both been shaped by and often aligned with much of what has been popular with millennials over the past 15 years—from *Girls* to Grumpy Cat to Rhianna to an unfortunate period between 2005 and 2006 in which I wore absurdly oversized eyeglasses. It was a shameful attempt to be fashionable.

And yet I'm set apart from Generation Y too. I didn't have a cell phone until I was 30. Not only do I remember a time before the Internet, but the Internet was not a daily part of my life until I was well into my undergraduate degree. I grew up in a town of 80 people. I'm more tech savvy than many of my older colleagues and family members, but I don't use Snapchat or Instagram. I have 28 Facebook friends, most of whom I'm related to. A student once referred to me as "a friendly social media dinosaur."

A more meaningful separation between my perspective and that of most millennials is that I ended up with a good job shortly after finishing school. Sure, I worked hard at my research, and I'm passionate about teaching. But millions of millennials work harder than I do and are no less passionate, and they don't have the secure, well-paying job with the independence and prestige that I do. As a white man with Canadian citizenship and a middle-class background, I've enjoyed all sorts of privileges throughout my life that aren't available to people whose identities locate them differently within social hierarchies. Of course lots of disadvantaged people overcome odds against them and thrive. The point is that while my career success at times feels like the result of a lottery—I just happened to be in the right place at the right time—it's a lottery in which I was holding a great many more tickets than most millennials on account of my many unearned privileges.

Unless gains are soon made by movements for more expansive social and economic rights, I may be part of the last cohort of workers who end up in well-paying, secure jobs with good benefits and a pension. This sets me apart from people my age and younger; but it also binds me to them, precisely because I'm an exception to the rule.

So when I say that my relationship with the millennial generation is complicated, it's because I'm approaching it both as an insider and an outsider. I'm almost the same age as the oldest millennials, and I've been formed by millennial trends and friends. Yet, as a professor, I engage with millennials not as peers but as a teacher, an advisor, and at times a mentor. I've been humbled by students who tell me I'm approachable and easier to relate to than they expected. I assume this is partially because of my age and partially because when I show YouTube clips in class I'm usually able to navigate the Internet without too much trouble. But the fact remains that I am not only distant from millennial students in terms of the position of authority I hold, but in terms of my exceptionally fortunate career experience, which most of them will not attain if current trends aren't changed.

I have approached the issues in this book with a commitment to social scientific rigor. I care deeply about the stakes of the debate over millennial entitlement, but I've channeled my feelings into a process of inquiry guided by the methodical movement between rigorous fact-finding and explanation using the frameworks of formal social theory. Nevertheless, I don't hesitate to say that my interest in these issues is rooted in a sense of responsibility to use my privileged place in the university to communicate and contribute to the work of social movements for a new world of genuine democracy, social justice, and ecological sustainability.

GLOSSARY

The word *entitlement* carries different meanings and can be used in contradictory ways. Because the term is contested, and because my use of it varies, concise definitions of key technical uses of *entitlement* are provided below.

democratic entitlement A form of deservingness that facilitates social equity and deep democracy. Senses and institutions of democratic entitlement broaden access to wealth and power throughout society. For example, in the early part of the twentieth century, a collective sense of democratic entitlement drove women in many Western countries to fight for the right to vote. Institutions that protect democratic entitlement include, for example, universally accessible health care systems in Canada, the United Kingdom, Cuba, and Norway.

disentitlement The loss of existing entitlements, whether through changes to law or at the level of feeling. For example, in Canada, waged and unwaged workers have been disentitled by government cuts to welfare programs and growing barriers to unemployment benefits. People of color in the United States have described feeling disentitled of their safety and sense of self-worth after watching police go unpunished for killing unarmed young black men.

Rising fossil fuel production is a source of ecological disentitlement. The legal authority of resource extraction corporations
effectively disentitles humans and all living things of sustainable
futures on Earth.

entitlement Defined by the Oxford English Dictionary (OED 2016a)
as "a legal right or just claim to do, receive, or possess something." In
the field of psychology, however, entitlement is an indicator of narcissism. Psychologists who apply the term to the millennial generation define being entitled as holding unreasonably high expectations
and acting as if you have a right to something even when you don't.
Yet the word can also refer to a government program or a general
feeling of deservingness. For example, social security benefits are an
entitlement of all US citizens. Black Lives Matter protestors describe
feeling entitled to better treatment by police. The term *entitlement*,
then, is a field of contestation. It is contested not only because it can
be used to refer to both legitimate and illegitimate claims of deservingness, but also because there are major disputes about where to
draw the line between legitimate and illegitimate entitlement claims.
Is it fair or excessive for students to demand free college tuition?
How conceptions of entitlement take shape in common sense depends on the state of struggles among social groups.

legal entitlements Laws, conventions, and other institutions that
codify who is entitled to what resources, and who is entitled to feel
what in a specific time and place. In the United States today, core
legal entitlements include social security, Medicare, public education, and compensation for the unemployed. (None of these legal
entitlements existed 150 years ago.) If you are an American citizen,
you are legally entitled to access the supports provided by these
programs. The legal frameworks of modern liberal democracies
entitle citizens to free speech. In a capitalist economic system, individuals and corporations are entitled to privately own and use
key productive resources to generate private profit. While there
is no law stating that people are entitled to breathe air without
paying for it, it is a widely held custom that breathing oxygen is

free. These and other deeply established customs can be considered legal entitlements.

myth of the age of entitlement (or age of entitlement narrative) A widely circulating, general storyline that portrays millennials, also known as members of "Generation Y," as more excessively entitled than any previous generation. (Millennials are people born between the early 1980s and the early 2000s.) According to the myth, the age of entitlement was created by some combination of bad parenting methods, narcissist-inducing digital and new media technologies, and the celebration of entitled behavior in popular culture. These and other phenomena have caused millennials to develop inflated expectations about what they deserve, even though they have been given so much. The excessive entitlement of Generation Y is portrayed as a threat to society. The overarching storyline is a myth because, despite being repeated often and broadly accepted as truth, it is both inaccurate and an obstacle to understanding crucial realities about millennial experiences.

oppressive entitlement A form of deservingness that draws on and strengthens existing social hierarchies. Senses and institutions of oppressive entitlement defend and extend systematically unequal access to wealth and power across society. For example, to suggest that in today's society everyone has the same chance to succeed, regardless of skin color, defends the oppressive entitlements of white people in a society where anti-black racism is widespread. Institutions that reproduce oppressive entitlement include state and business policies ensuring that small numbers of people will be rich while most people will struggle to achieve basic living standards.

politics of entitlement A term designed to draw attention to the fact that labeling ideas and behavior as "excessively entitled" always involves struggles over social power. There is no such thing as a society with "no entitlement." Every society is organized around formal and informal rules governing who is entitled to access what resources, and who is entitled to feel what. The shape of those rules reflect the state of struggles between groups with competing interests. The myth of the age of entitlement ignores the politics of entitlement by uncritically assuming that certain expressions of deservingness are overly entitled, while other claims of deservingness are normal or not entitled. For example, the entry-level millennial employee who expects a living salary is called entitled. The employer who expects millennial workers to hustle obediently in hopes of renewing their low-wage, short-term contract is called a good businessperson. The myth portrays college students as overly entitled for demanding changes to curriculum that would include the experiences of marginalized people. What the myth leaves out, however, is that the defenders of the status quo are similarly making an entitlement claim: They feel entitled to teach courses that exclude the experiences of marginalized people. The difference is that by defending existing relationships of power, advocates of the status quo more easily portray their position as being reasonable, even natural. Focusing on the politics of entitlement helps clarify the deservingness claims on all sides. It draws attention to the social context in which behaviors and policies become perceived as excessive or normal. More fully addressing the politics of entitlement involves asking who deserves access to what resources, and who deserves to feel what?

real entitlement framework A concept that helps to envision the overall balance of who is entitled to access what resources and who is entitled to feel what in a particular time and place. The concept is not intended to compare the entitlement of different social groups with statistical precision; however, it encourages reflecting on the fact that legal entitlements exist within a sprawling network of protections and exclusions. Each particular legal entitlement, while being significant on its own, is also part of a larger whole, an overarching sociolegal framework that shapes the opportunities and limits within which lives are lived by individuals and groups. We can imagine the framework as relatively stable at any given moment, yet it changes in relation to social struggles. For example, as discussed in Chapter 3, in the early decades of the twentieth century the real entitlement framework in advanced capitalist countries protected the rights of employers and investors far more robustly than the rights of workers. In the mid-twentieth century, pressure from mass labor movements changed the shape of the real entitlement framework. By the 1960s, workers had won crucial new rights and protections that altered the balance of forces as reflected in and reproduced by the real entitlement framework of that period. Since the 1970s, neoliberal state and business policies have rolled back workers' gains and social rights, tilting the balance of power entrenched in the real entitlement framework back toward employers, investors, and large financial interests.

senses of entitlement Feelings of deservingness, whether the thing one feels deserving of has been attained or not. For example, black slaves who resisted bondage before emancipation were driven by shared senses of being entitled to freedom. Today, workers feel entitled to be paid a set amount in exchange for work they perform for an employer—and indeed, this right is enshrined in labor law. However, in practice, many workers, especially migrant workers, despite feeling entitled to fair pay, are grossly underpaid. In other words, senses of entitlement exist in relation to, but are not reducible to, official rules articulated by legal entitlements. Senses of entitlement can be democratic or oppressive. Employers paying migrant workers less than the cost of domestic labor feel entitled to profit from inequalities embedded in global capitalism. Their sense of entitlement is oppressive. Migrant workers demanding equitable and just working and living conditions are driven by senses of democratic entitlement.

REFERENCES

Ablow, Keith. 2013. "We Are Raising a Generation of Deluded Narcissists." *Fox News*, January 8. http://www.foxnews.com/opinion/2013/01/08/are-raising-generation-deluded-narcissists.html.

Ahmed, Sara. 2014a. "Feminist Hurt/Feminism Hurts." *feministkilljoys: A Wilfulness Archive*, July 21. https://feministkilljoys.com/2014/07/21/feminist-hurtfeminism-hurts/.

Ahmed, Sara. 2014b. *Willful Subjects*. Durham: Duke University Press.

Ahmed, Sara. 2015. "Against Students." *New Inquiry*, June 29. http://thenewinquiry.com/essays/against-students/.

Alba, Davey. 2015. "Startup Aims to Make Silicon Valley an Actual Meritocracy." *Wired*, May 27. https://www.wired.com/2015/05/gradberry-tara-ai/.

Alexander, Michelle. 2010. *The New Jim Crow: Mass Incarceration in the Age of Colorblindness*. New York: The New Press.

Alsop, Ron. 2008. *The Trophy Kids Grow Up: How the Millennial Generation Is Shaking Up the Workplace*. San Francisco: Jossey-Bass.

Alter, Charlotte. 2015. "Millennials Are Setting New Records—For Living with Their Parents." *Time*, November 11. http://time.com/4108515/millennials-live-at-home-parents/.

Amnesty International. 2016. "Economic and Social Rights." http://www.amnesty.ca/our-work/issues/economic-and-social-rights.

Andersen, Erika. 2016. "Why You're Having a Hard Time with Your Millennial Employees—And What to Do About It." *Forbes*, May 9. https://www.forbes.com/sites/erikaandersen/2016/05/09/why-youre-having-a-hard-time-with-your-millenial-employees-and-what-to-do-about-it/#6b9d470333aa.

Anderson, Kirk. 2016. "'The Gig Economy,' The Early Years." *Forbes*, March 31. https://www.forbes.com/sites/cartoonoftheday/2016/03/31/gig-economy-silicon-valley-uber-labor-benefits-ayn-rand-cartoon/#175a97f23ac8.

Anderson, Nick, and Scott Clement. 2015. "1 in 5 College Women Say They Were Violated." *Washington Post*, June 12. https://www.washingtonpost.com/news/fact-checker/wp/2014/12/17/one-in-five-women-in-college-sexually-assaulted-an-update/.

Aschoff, Nicole. 2015. *The New Prophets of Capital*. London: Verso.

Aspen Group. 2012. "Narcissistic and Entitled to Everything! Does Gen Y Have Too Much Self-Esteem?" http://aspeneducation.crchealth.com/articles/article-entitlement/.

Atlanta Journal-Constitution. 2016. "John Lewis on Bernie Sanders: 'There's Not Anything Free in America." February 17. http://politics.blog.myajc.com/2016/02/17/john-lewis-on-bernie-sanders-nothing-free-in-america/.

Barr, Caelainn, and Shiv Malik. 2016. "Revealed: The 30-Year Economic Betrayal Dragging Down Generation Y's Income." *Guardian*, March 7. https://www.theguardian.com/world/2016/mar/07/revealed-30-year-economic-betrayal-dragging-down-generation-y-income.

Beccaro, Clara, and Supriya Ganesh. 2016. "Feminist to the Core." *Columbia Spectator*, March 24. http://columbiaspectator.com/opinion/2016/03/24/feminist-core.

Bell, Daniel. 1975. "The Revolution of Rising Entitlements." *Fortune*, April, 98–103, 182, 185.

Benanav, Aaron. 2015. "Precarity Rising." *Viewpoint*, June 15. https://viewpointmag.com/2015/06/15/precarity-rising/.

Bentley University. 2014. "Millennials at Work." A Bentley University–commissioned study, November 11. http://www.bentley.edu/newsroom/latest-headlines/mind-of-millennial.

Berlant, Lauren. 2011. *Cruel Optimism*. Durham: Duke University Press. http://dx.doi.org/10.1215/9780822394716.

Bisceglia, Sean. 2014. "Outside Opinion: Millennials Frustrate HR Execs." *Chicago Tribune*, September 5. http://www.chicagotribune.com/business/ct-hiring-millennials-outside-opinion-0907-biz-20140905-story.html.

Black Lives Matter. 2016. "About the Black Lives Matter Network." http://blacklivesmatter.com/about/.

Blades, Meteor. 2015. "Inflation-Adjusted Wages Have Declined Since Great Recession, and Worse for Low-Wage Occupations." *AlterNet*, September 10. http://www.alternet.org/economy/inflation-adjusted-wages-have-declined-great-recession-and-worse-low-wage-occupations.

Blake, Aaron. 2016. "More Young People Voted for Bernie Sanders than Trump and Clinton Combined—By a Lot." *Washington Post*, June 20. https://www.washingtonpost.com/news/the-fix/wp/2016/06/20/more-young-people-voted-for-bernie-sanders-than-trump-and-clinton-combined-by-a-lot/.

Boesveld, Sarah. 2014. "'I Bought My Degree, Now I Want My Job!' Entitled Students on Fast Track to Becoming Disgruntled Employees: Study." *National Post*, May 25. http://news.nationalpost.com/news/canada/i-bought-my-degree-now-i-want-my-job-entitled-students-on-fast-track-to-becoming-disgruntled-employees-study.

Boryga, Andrew. 2016. "These Struggling Twentysomethings Have Never Even Heard of 'Millennials.'" *Fusion*, February 2. http://fusion.net/story/266611/struggling-twenty-somethings-have-never-even-heard-of-millennials/.

Bowles, Samuel, and Herbert Gintis. 1976. *Schooling in Capitalist America: Educational Reform and the Contradictions of Economic Life*. New York: Basic Books.

Bowles, Samuel, and Herbert Gintis. 1982. "The Crisis of Liberal Democratic Capitalism: The Case of the United States." *Politics & Society* 11(1): 51–93. http://dx.doi.org/10.1177/003232928201100103.

Britto Schwartz, Juliana. 2016. "Becoming 'Water Protectors' Changed Their Lives." *CNN.com*, October 27. http://www.cnn.com/2016/10/27/opinions/youth-against-dakota-pipeline-britto-schwartz/.

Brooks, Arthur. 2015. "Choose to Be Grateful. It Will Make You Happier." *New York Times*, November 21. https://www.nytimes.com/2015/11/22/opinion/sunday/choose-to-be-grateful-it-will-make-you-happier.html?_r=0.

Brooks, David. 2015. "The Structure of Gratitude." *New York Times*, July 28. https://www.nytimes.com/2015/07/28/opinion/david-brooks-the-structure-of-gratitude.html.

Bureau of Investigative Journalism. 2016. "Get the Data: Drone Wars." https://www.thebureauinvestigates.com/category/projects/drones/drones-graphs/.

Burrell, Brian, and Reid Setzer. 2015. "Through Their Eyes: The Challenges Facing Young Workers in California's Post-Recession Economy." *Young Invincibles*, May 7. http://younginvincibles.org/wp-content/uploads/2015/05/Through-Their-Eyes-May72015.pdf.

Buskey, Nikki. 2010. "Bayou Lafourche, 'The Longest Main Street in the World.'" *Houma Today*, February 15. http://www.houmatoday.com/article/20100215/LIVING03/100219554.

Butler, David. 2006. *Enterprise Planning and Development: Small Business Start-up, Survival and Development*. London: Routledge.

Cairns, James. 2015. "Common Sense on Campus: Disaffected Consent in the Age of Austerity." *Studies in Political Economy* 96(1): 123–44. http://dx.doi.org/10.1080/19187033.2015.11674940.

Cairns, James, and Alan Sears. 2012. *The Democratic Imagination: Envisioning Popular Power in the Twenty-First Century*. Toronto: University of Toronto Press.

Cairns, Kate. 2012. "Partnering Power: Questions Posed from Governmentality." In *Canadian Education: Governing Practices & Producing Subjects*, edited by Brenda L. Spencer, Kenneth D. Gariepy, Kari Dehli, and James Ryan, 37–56. Calgary: Sense Publishers. http://dx.doi.org/10.1007/978-94-6091-861-2_4.

Canadian Federation of Students. 2013. "Funding for Post-Secondary Education." http://cfs-fcee.ca/wp-content/uploads/sites/2/2013/11/Fact-Sheet-Funding-2013-11-En.pdf.

Carrick, Rob. 2012. "2012 vs. 1984: Young Adults Really Do Have It Harder Today." *Globe and Mail*, December 18. http://www.theglobeandmail.com/globe-investor/personal-finance/2012-vs-1984-young-adults-really-do-have-it-harder-today/article4105604/.

Carrick, Rob. 2016. "Young People Are Right to Be Angry about Morneau's Acceptance of 'Job Churn.'" *Globe and Mail*, October 28. http://www.theglobeandmail.com/globe-investor/personal-finance/genymoney/why-morneau-needs-to-be-less-accepting-of-temporary-work/article32543380/.

Caruso, Charlie, ed. 2014. *Understanding Y: #andYyoushould*. Stafford: Wrightbooks.

Castellanos, Alex. 2015. "Mizzou, Yale and the Culture of Entitlement in Colleges." *CNN*, November 13. http://www.cnn.com/2015/11/13/opinions/castellanos-mizzou-yale-students/.

CBC News. 2013. "Idle No More Protesters Block QEII Highway." http://www.cbc.ca/news/canada/edmonton/idle-no-more-protesters-block-qeii-highway-1.1368673.

Chait, Jonathan. 2016. "The Case against Bernie Sanders." *New York Magazine*, January 18. http://nymag.com/daily/intelligencer/2016/01/case-against-bernie-sanders.html.

Charbonneau, Leo. 2011. "Enrolment Will Continue to Climb Despite Demographic Decline." *University Affairs*, May 26. http://www.universityaffairs.ca/news/news-article/enrolment-will-continue-to-climb-despite-demographic-decline-aspx.

Chomsky, Noam. 2015. "The United States, not Iran, Poses the Greatest Threat to World Peace." *Democracy Now*, September 22. https://www.democracynow.org/2015/9/22/noam_chomsky_the_united_states_not.

CLASSE. 2012. "Share Our Future: The CLASSE Manifesto." http://www.stopthehike.ca/2012/07/share-our-future-the-classe-manifesto/.

Coates, Ta-Nehisi. 2015. *Between the World and Me*. New York: Spiegel & Grau.

Cogin, Julie. 2012. "Are Generational Differences in Work Values Fact or Fiction? Multi-Country Evidence and Implications." *International Journal of Human Resource Management* 23(11): 2268–94. http://dx.doi.org/10.1080/09585192.2011.610967.

Confessore, Nicholas. 2016. "For Whites Sensing Decline, Donald Trump Unleashes Words of Resistance." *New York Times*, July 13. https://www.nytimes.com/2016/07/14/us/politics/donald-trump-white-identity.html.

Connell, R.W. 2014. *Masculinities* (2nd ed.) Berkeley: University of California Press.

Council of Ontario Universities. 2013. "Entrepreneurship at Ontario Universities: Fuelling Success." http://cou.on.ca/wp-content/uploads/2015/05/COU-Entrepreneurship-Fuelling-Success-2013.pdf.

Cote, James E., and Anton L. Allahar. 2007. *Ivory Tower Blues: A University System in Crisis*. Toronto: University of Toronto Press.

Court, Emma. 2016. "'Fickle' Millennials Blamed for Chipotle's Downward Spiral." *MarketWatch*, March 18. http://www.marketwatch.com/story/chipotle-stock-drops-after-rare-bearish-call-at-jefferies-2016-03-17.

Covert, Bryce. 2016. "Bernie's Revolution vs. Hillary's Getting Things Done." *New York Times*, February 1. https://www.nytimes.com/2016/02/01/opinion/campaign-stops/bernies-revolution-vs-hillarys-getting-things-done.html?_r=0.

Cowburn, Ashley. 2016. "George Osborne to Use Cut in Disability Benefits to 'Fund Middle-Class Tax Giveaway.'" *Independent*, March 12. http://www.independent.co.uk/news/uk/politics/budget-2016-george-osborne-to-use-a-cut-in-benefit-payments-to-disabled-people-to-fund-a-middle-a6927056.html.

Crockett, Emily, and StudentNation. 2013. "Why Millennials Aren't Lazy, Entitled Narcissists: A Response to *Time* Magazine's Joel Stein." *The*

Nation, May 16. https://www.thenation.com/article/why-millennials-arent-lazy-entitled-narcissists/.

Cronin, Brenda. 2013. "Some 95% of 2009–2012 Income Gains Went to Wealthiest 1%." *Wall Street Journal*, September 10. http://blogs.wsj.com/economics/2013/09/10/some-95-of-2009-2012-income-gains-went-to-wealthiest-1/.

Cuomo, Andrew M. 2016. "Governor Cuomo Signs $15 Minimum Wage Plan and 12 Week Paid Family Leave Policy into Law." New York State, April 4. https://www.governor.ny.gov/news/governor-cuomo-signs-15-minimum-wage-plan-and-12-week-paid-family-leave-policy-law.

Davis, Alyssa, and Lawrence Mishel. 2014. "CEO Pay Continues to Rise as Typical Workers Are Paid Less." Economic Policy Institute, Issue Brief #380, June 12. http://www.epi.org/publication/ceo-pay-continues-to-rise/.

Davis, Angela. 2003. *Are Prisons Obsolete?* New York: Seven Stories Press.

Dawson, Mackenzie. 2015. "STFU Millennials: 5 Easy Ways Not to Act Entitled." *New York Post*, April 27. http://nypost.com/2015/04/27/hey-millennials-here-are-5-easy-ways-not-to-act-entitled/.

Dean, Malcolm. 2013. "Margaret Thatcher's Policies Hit the Poor Hardest: And It's Happening Again." *Guardian*, April 9. https://www.theguardian.com/society/2013/apr/09/margaret-thatcher-policies-poor-society.

deBoer, Fredrik. 2016. "Hillary Clinton Lost. Bernie Sanders Could Have Won." *Washington Post*, November 10. https://www.washingtonpost.com/posteverything/wp/2016/11/10/hillary-clinton-lost-bernie-sanders-could-have-won/?utm_term=.8b778b0f31bf.

Delwiche, Theodore R., and Mariel A. Klein. 2015. "Divest Harvard Ends 'Heat Week' Protests." *Harvard Crimson*, April 18. http://www.thecrimson.com/article/2015/4/18/divest-harvard-ends-protests/?utm_source=thecrimson&utm_medium=web_primary&utm_campaign=recommend_sidebar.

Democracy Now. 2012. "On Strike! Fast-Food Workers in NYC Call for Right to Unionize." https://www.democracynow.org/blog/2012/11/30/video_on_strike_fast_food_workers_in_nyc_call_for_right_to_unionize.

Democracy Now. 2015. "Black Student Revolt Against Racism Ousts 2 Top Officials at University of Missouri." https://www.democracynow.org/2015/11/10/black_student_uprising_over_racial_bias.

Derber, Charles. 1978. "Unemployment and the Entitled Worker: Job-Entitlement and Radical Political Attitudes among the Youthful Unemployed." *Social Problems* 26(1): 26–37. http://dx.doi.org/10.2307/800430.

Desilver, Drew. 2013. "U.S. Income Inequality, on Rise for Decades, Is Now Highest Since 1928." Pew Research Center, December 5. http://www.pewresearch.org/fact-tank/2013/12/05/u-s-income-inequality-on-rise-for-decades-is-now-highest-since-1928/.

Divest Harvard. 2016. "Home." http://divestharvard.com/.

Drake, Bruce. 2014. "6 New Findings about Millennials." Pew Research Center, March 7. http://www.pewresearch.org/fact-tank/2014/03/07/6-new-findings-about-millennials/.

Dreifus, Claudia. 2011. "A Conversation with Samantha B. Joye." *New York Times*, March 22. http://query.nytimes.com/gst/fullpage.html?res=9500E4DD1531F931A15750C0A9679D8B63.

Dombek, Kristin. 2016. *The Selfishness of Others: An Essay on the Fear of Narcissism*. New York: Farrar, Straus and Giroux.

Duke, Brendan. 2016. "When I Was Your Age: Millennials and the Generational Wage Gap." Center for American Progress, March 3. https://www.americanprogress.org/issues/economy/report/2016/03/03/131627/when-i-was-your-age/.

Durkin, J.D. 2016. "Pollster Frank Luntz: If You're a Young Millennial Socialist You're Totally Getting Laid Tonight." *Mediaite*, February 12. http://www.mediaite.com/online/pollster-frank-luntz-if-youre-a-young-millennial-socialist-youre-totally-getting-laid-tonight/.

Eagleton, Terry. 2015. *Hope without Optimism*. Charlottesville: University of Virginia Press.

Eberstadt, Nicholas. 2012. *A Nation of Takers: America's Entitlement Epidemic*. West Conshohocken: Templeton Press.

Economic Policy Institute. 2015. "The Productivity–Pay Gap." September. http://www.epi.org/productivity-pay-gap/.

Eidelson, Josh, and Sarah Jaffe. 2013. "Fast Food Nation." Belabored Podcast #17, August 6. https://www.dissentmagazine.org/blog/belabored-podcast-17-fast-food-nation-2.

Ekins, Emily. 2014. "The Millennials: The Politically Unclaimed Generation." *The Reason-Rupe Spring 2014 Millennial Survey*, July 10. http://reason.com/assets/db/14048862817887.pdf.

Eyre, Richard, and Linda Eyre. 2011. *The Entitlement Trap: How to Rescue Your Child with a New Family System of Choosing, Earning, and Ownership*. New York: Penguin.

Federici, Silvia. 1975. *Wages against Housework*. Bristol: Falling Wall Press.

Feminist Campus. 2016. "Campaign to End Campus Sexual Violence." http://feministcampus.org/campaigns/campus-violence/.

Ferguson, Sue, and David McNally. 2015. "Social Reproduction beyond Intersectionality: An Interview." *Viewpoint*, October 31. https://viewpointmag.com/2015/10/31/social-reproduction-beyond-intersectionality-an-interview-with-sue-ferguson-and-david-mcnally/.

Fiedler, Katharina. 2015. "90% of American Workers Don't Own Their Own Business, Rick Santorum Says." *Politifact*, April 13. http://www.politifact.com/truth-o-meter/statements/2015/apr/13/rick-santorum/90-american-workers-dont-own-their-own-business-ri/.

Finkel, Alvin. 2014. "Workers' Social-Wage Struggles During the Great Depression and the Era of Neoliberalism: International Comparisons." In *Workers in Hard Times: A Long View of Economic Crises*, edited by Leon Fink, Joseph A. McCartin, and Joan Sangster, 113–40. Urbana-Champaign: University of Illinois Press.

Finkelman, Peter. 2006. "*Scott v. Sandford*: The Court's Most Dreadful Case and How It Changed History." *Chicago-Kent Law Review* 82(1): 3–48.

Finnegan, William. 2014. "Dignity: Fast-Food Workers and a New Form of Labor Activism." *New Yorker*, September 15. http://www.newyorker.com/magazine/2014/09/15/dignity-4.

Foreman, Amanda. 2014. "Feckless, Spoilt, Lazy … Now Where Did Our Millennials Learn That?" *Sunday Times* (London), July 27. http://www.thesundaytimes.co.uk/sto/comment/columns/article1438901.ece.

Foster, John Bellamy. 2000. *Marx's Ecology: Materialism and Nature.* New York: Monthly Review Press.

Fottrell, Quentin. 2015. "A College Degree Is Worth $1 Million." *MarketWatch*, May 8. http://www.marketwatch.com/story/a-college-degree-is-worth-1-million-2015-05-07.

Freeman, Richard, Eunice Han, David Madland, and Brendan Duke. 2015. "Bargaining for the American Dream: What Unions Do for Mobility." Center for American Progress, September 9. https://www.americanprogress.org/issues/economy/report/2015/09/09/120558/bargaining-for-the-american-dream/.

Friedman, Jaclyn, and Jessica Valenti. 2008. *Yes Means Yes! Visions of Female Sexual Power & a World without Rape.* Berkeley: Seal Press.

Frumkin, Paul. 2012. "NYC Quick-Service Workers Strike for Higher Wages, Unions." *Nation's Restaurant News*, November 29. http://nrn.com/latest-headlines/nyc-quick-service-workers-strike-higher-wages-unions.

Garside, Juliette. 2015. "Recession Rich: Britain's Wealthiest Double Net Worth Since Crisis." *Guardian*, April 26. https://www.theguardian.com/business/2015/apr/26/recession-rich-britains-wealthiest-double-net-worth-since-crisis.

Garza, Alicia. 2014. "A Herstory of the #BlackLivesMatter Movement." *Feminist Wire*, October 7. http://www.thefeministwire.com/2014/10/blacklivesmatter-2/.

Gaztambide-Fernández, Rubén, Kate Cairns, and Chandni Desai. 2013. "The Sense of Entitlement." In *Privilege, Agency, and Affect*, edited by P. Aggleton and C. Maxwell, 32–49. Basingstoke: Palgrave Macmillan. http://dx.doi.org/10.1057/9781137292636_3.

Geobey, Sean. 2013. "The Young and the Jobless: Youth Unemployment in Ontario." Canadian Centre for Policy Alternatives, September 27. https://www.policyalternatives.ca/publications/reports/young-and-jobless.

Gillespie, Nick. 2015. "Trigger Warning: College Kids Are Human Veal." *Daily Beast*, April 30. http://www.thedailybeast.com/articles/2015/04/30/trigger-warning-college-kids-are-human-veal.html.

Gilson, Dave. 2011. "Overworked America: 12 Charts that Will Make Your Blood Boil." *Mother Jones*, July/August. http://www.motherjones.com/politics/2011/06/speedup-americans-working-harder-charts.

Giroux, Henry A. 2013. *Neoliberalism's War on Higher Education.* Toronto: Between the Lines.

Godderis, Rebecca, and Jennifer L. Root. 2016. "Trigger Warnings: Compassion Is Not Censorship." *Radical Pedagogy* 13(2): 130–8.

Goldring, Hugh. 2014. "Colonialism Bytes: A Review of 'Idle No More: Blockade.'" *Ad Astra*, July 23. https://adastracomix.com/2014/07/23/colonialism-bytes-a-review-of-idle-no-more-blockade/.

Goodman, Amy. 2014. "Black Youth-Organized Millions March NYC Draws Tens of Thousands in Movement's Biggest Protest Yet." *Democracy Now*, December 15. http://www.democracynow.org/2014/12/15/black_youth_organized_millions_march_nyc.

Gramsci, Antonio. 1971. *Selections from the Prison Notebooks.* Edited and translated by Quintin Hoare and Geoffrey Nowell-Smith. New York: International Publishers.

Graeber, David. 2013. *The Democracy Project: A History, a Crisis, a Movement*. New York: Spiegel & Grau.

Grant, Tavia. 2014. "The 15-Hour Workweek: Canada's Part-Time Problem." *Globe and Mail*, October 4, B6–7.

Graves, Jada A. 2012. "Millennial Workers: Entitled, Needy, Self-Centered?" *U.S. News*, June 27. http://money.usnews.com/money/careers/articles/2012/06/27/millennial-workers-entitled-needy-self-centered.

Greenberger, Ellen, Jared Lessard, Chuansheng Chen, and Susan P. Farruggia. 2008. "Self-Entitled College Students: Contributions of Personality, Parenting, and Motivational Factors." *Journal of Youth and Adolescence* 37(10): 1193–204. http://dx.doi.org/10.1007/s10964-008-9284-9.

Greenhouse, Steven. 2012. "With Day of Protests, Fast-Food Workers Seek More Pay." *New York Times*, November 29. http://www.nytimes.com/2012/11/30/nyregion/fast-food-workers-in-new-york-city-rally-for-higher-wages.html.

Greenhouse, Steven, and Jana Kasperkevic. 2015. "Fight for $15 Swells into Largest Protest by Low-Wage Workers in US History." *Guardian*, April 15. https://www.theguardian.com/us-news/2015/apr/15/fight-for-15-minimum-wage-protests-new-york-los-angeles-atlanta-boston.

Griswold, Alex. 2015. "Donald Trump: Bernie Sanders Is a 'Maniac' and 'Communist.'" *Mediaite*, October 15. http://www.mediaite.com/online/donald-trump-bernie-sanders-is-a-maniac-and-communist/.

Gude, Shawn. 2013. "In Defence of Entitlements." *Jacobin*, December 17. https://www.jacobinmag.com/2013/12/in-defense-of-entitlements/.

Gupta-Sunderji, Merge. 2014. "Want Respect, Millennials? Here's How to Earn It." *Globe and Mail*, June 10. http://www.theglobeandmail.com/report-on-business/careers/leadership-lab/want-respect-millennials-heres-how-to-earn-it/article19075712/.

Hanchard, Michael. 2015. "State Violence Against Black and Brown Youth." *Huffington Post*, June 9. http://www.huffingtonpost.com/michael-hanchard/state-violence-against-black-and-brown-youth_b_7000210.html.

Hardgrove, Abby, Linda McDowell, and Esther Rootham. 2015. "Precarious Lives, Precarious Labour: Family Support and Young Men's Transitions to Work in the UK." *Journal of Youth Studies* 18(8): 1057–76. http://dx.doi.org/10.1080/13676261.2015.1020933.

Harris, Malcolm. 2015. "There Is No College Bubble." *The Awl*, October 27. http://www.theawl.com/2015/10/there-is-no-college-bubble.

Harry, Sydette. 2013. "Not All Millennials Are White and Privileged!" *Salon*, October 18. http://www.salon.com/2013/10/18/not_all_millennials_are_white_and_privileged/.

Harvey, David. 2007. *A Brief History of Neoliberalism*. New York: Oxford University Press.

Hayward, Steven F. 2015. "The EPA Doubles Down: Its Latest Regulations Show an Agency Captured by Environmental Activists." *Weekly Standard*, August 17. http://www.weeklystandard.com/epa-doubles-down/article/1006574?page=1.

Heathfield, Susan M. 2015. "The Downside of Hiring Generation Y." *About Money*, January 25. https://humanresources.about.com/od/generations-at-work/a/downside-of-hiring-generation-y.htm.

Hedges, Chris. 2015. *Wages of Rebellion: The Moral Imperatives of Revolt*. New York: Nation Books.

Henderson, Alex. 2013. "10 Reasons Millennials Are the Screwed Generation." *Alternet*, September 12. http://www.alternet.org/corporate-accountability-and-workplace/10-reasons-millennials-are-screwed-generation.

Hickman, Blair. 2014. "What We Learned Investigating Unpaid Internships." *ProPublica*, July 23. https://www.propublica.org/article/what-we-learned-investigating-unpaid-internships.

hooks, bell. 1988. *Talking Back: Thinking Feminist, Thinking Black*. Toronto: Between the Lines.

Howe, Neil, and William Strauss. 2000. *Millennials Rising: The Next Great Generation*. New York: Vintage Books.

Idle No More. 2013. "The Vision." http://www.idlenomore.ca/vision.

Ignatius, David. 2016. "Bernie Sanders Needs to Get Serious on Foreign Policy." *Washington Post*, February 11. https://www.washingtonpost.com/opinions/what-would-be-the-sanders-doctrine/2016/02/11/140bbd62-d103-11e5-b2bc-988409ee911b_story.html.

Ihaza, Jeff. 2016. "What Does a Millennial Look Like?" *Awl*, April 20. https://theawl.com/what-does-a-millennial-look-like-ae148c2a1ee#.hst7mui1c.

Imtiaz, Saba, and Zia ur-Rehman. 2015. "Death Toll from Heat Wave in Karachi, Pakistan, Hits 1,000." *New York Times*, June 25. https://www.nytimes.com/2015/06/26/world/asia/karachi-pakistan-heat-wave-deaths.html?_r=0.

Institute for College Access & Success. 2015. "Student Debt and the Class of 2014." Annual Report, October. http://ticas.org/sites/default/files/pdf/classof2014_embargoed.pdf.

Intergovernmental Panel on Climate Change. 2014. *Climate Change 2014: Synthesis Report*. http://www.ipcc.ch/report/ar5/syr/.

International Labour Organization. 2015. World Employment Social Outlook: The Changing Nature of Jobs. http://www.ilo.org/wcmsp5/groups/public/---dgreports/---dcomm/---publ/documents/publication/wcms_368626.pdf.

Izzo, Phil. 2014. "Congratulations to Class of 2014, Most Indebted Ever." *Wall Street Journal*, May 16. http://blogs.wsj.com/numbers/congatulations-to-class-of-2014-the-most-indebted-ever-1368/.

Johnson, Whitney. 2012. "Battling Entitlement, the Innovation-Killer." *Harvard Business Review*, January 12. http://hbr.org/2012/01/battling-entitlement-the-innov/.

Juhasz, Antonia. 2010. *Black Tide: The Devastating Impact of the Gulf Oil Spill*. New York: Wiley.

Kalleberg, Arne L. 2009. "Precarious Work, Insecure Workers: Employment Relations in Transition." *American Sociological Review* 74 (1): 1–22. http://dx.doi.org/10.1177/000312240907400101.

Kalleberg, Arne L. 2011. *Good Jobs, Bad Jobs: The Rise of Polarized and Precarious Employment Systems in the United States, 1970s–2000s*. New York: Russell Sage Foundation.

Kaufman, Micha. 2013. "The Gig Economy: The Force that Could Save the American Worker?" *Wired*, September. https://www.wired.com/insights/2013/09/the-gig-economy-the-force-that-could-save-the-american-worker/.

Kaufman, Micha. 2014. "Hate Your Job? Five Steps to Escape and Do What You Love." *Forbes*, March 21. https://www.forbes.com/sites/michakaufman/2014/03/21/hate-your-job-five-steps-to-escape-and-do-what-you-love/#779f26d86475.

Kaufmann, Bobby. 2016. "'Suck It Up', Buttercup' Lawmaker Hangs Up on *As It Happens*. Interview by Carol Off, CBC Radio 1, *As It Happens*, November 16. http://www.cbc.ca/radio/asithappens/as-it-happens-wednesday-edition-1.3853526/suck-it-up-buttercup-lawmaker-hangs-up-on-as-it-happens-1.3853530.

Kasperkevic, Jana. 2015. "Fight for $15: Workers across US Protest to Raise Minimum Wage—As It Happened." *Guardian*, April 15. https://www.theguardian.com/us-news/live/2015/apr/15/fight-for-15-protest-workers-minimum-wage-live.

Katsiaficas, George. 1987. *The Imagination of the New Left: A Global Analysis of 1968*. Boston: South End Press.

Katsiaficas, George. 2006. *The Subversion of Politics: European Autonomous Social Movements and the Decolonization of Everyday Life*. Oakland: AK Press.

Keane, Martin. 2000. "Social Rights: A Literature Review." Unpublished working paper for the Combat Poverty Agency, July. http://www.combatpoverty.ie/publications/SocialRightsALiteratureReview_2000.pdf.

Kelley, Robin D.G. 2002. *Freedom Dreams: The Black Radical Imagination*. Boston: Beacon Press.

Kessler, Sarah. 2014. "Pixel & Dimed: On (Not) Getting By in the Gig Economy." *Fast Company*, March 18. https://www.fastcompany.com/3027355/pixel-and-dimed-on-not-getting-by-in-the-gig-economy.

Keylor, William. 2013. "The Long-Forgotten Racial Attitudes and Policies of Woodrow Wilson." *Boston University Public Relations*, March 4. http://www.bu.edu/professorvoices/2013/03/04/the-long-forgotten-racial-attitudes-and-policies-of-woodrow-wilson/.

Klein, Naomi. 2014. *This Changes Everything: Capitalism vs. the Climate*. London: Allen Lane.

Knafo, Saki. 2013. "When It Comes to Illegal Drug Use, White America Does the Crime, Black America Gets the Time." *Huffington Post*, September 17. http://www.huffingtonpost.com/2013/09/17/racial-disparity-drug-use_n_3941346.html.

Know Your IX. 2016. "About KYIX." http://knowyourix.org/about-ky9/.

Kochhar, Rakesh, and Richard Fry. 2014. "Wealth Inequality Has Widened along Racial, Ethnic Lines Since End of Great Recession." Pew Research Center, October 12. http://www.pewresearch.org/fact-tank/2014/12/12/racial-wealth-gaps-great-recession/.

Kohn, Sally. 2016. "Bernie Sanders Is This Year's Biggest Story." CNN, March 29. http://www.cnn.com/2016/03/29/opinions/bernie-sanders-big-story-2016-opinion-kohn/.

Kopp, Jason P., Tracy E. Zinn, Sara J. Finney, and Daniel P. Jurich. 2011. "The Development and Evaluation of the Academic Entitlement Questionnaire." *Measurement & Evaluation in Counseling & Development* 44(2): 105–29. http://dx.doi.org/10.1177/0748175611400292.

Kotlikoff, Laurence. 2015. "The Budget Deal's Devastating Social Security Benefit Cuts." *Forbes*, October 28. https://www.forbes.com/sites/

kotlikoff/2015/10/28/the-house-budgets-devastating-social-security-benefit-cuts/#508ffc642be2.

Krueger, Alyson. 2014. "5 Things Every Boss Should Know about Working with Millennials." *Forbes*, April 10. https://www.forbes.com/sites/alysonkrueger/2014/04/10/5-things-every-boss-should-know-about-working-with-millennials/.

Krugman, Paul. 2016. "Obama's War on Inequality." *New York Times*, May 20. https://www.nytimes.com/2016/05/20/opinion/obamas-war-on-inequality.html?_r=0.

Kunkel, Benjamin. 2014. *Utopia or Bust: A Guide to the Present Crisis*. New York: Verso.

Lafrenière, Ginette. 2015. "Study by Laurier Researchers into Gendered Violence on Campus Shapes University Efforts to Change Culture and Improve Services." Wilfrid Laurier University Press Release, March 10. https://www.wlu.ca/media/news-releases/march-2015/study-by-laurier-researchers-into-gendered-violence-on-campus-shapes-university-efforts-to-change-culture-and-improve-services.html.

Lapowsky, Issie. 2016. "Clinton Tackles Tech's Biggest Issues in New Policy Agenda." *Wired*, June 28. https://www.wired.com/2016/06/clinton-wants-forgive-student-debt-entrepreneurs/.

Laxer, James. 2009. *Democracy*. Toronto: Groundwood.

LeBaron, Genevieve. 2014. "Reconceptualizing Debt Bondage: Debt as a Class-Based Form of Labor Discipline." *Critical Sociology* 40(5): 763–80. http://dx.doi.org/10.1177/0896920513512695.

Lebowitz, Michael A. 1977/78. "Capital and the Production of Needs." *Science and Society* 41(4): 430–47.

Lebowitz, Michael A. 2010. *The Socialist Alternative: Real Human Development*. New York: Monthly Review Press.

Legion of Black Collegians. 2015. "We Are No Longer Taking It. It's Time to Fight." @MizzouLBC, November 7. https://twitter.com/mizzoulbc/status/663177684428566532.

Leonard, Sarah. 2016. "Introduction." In *The Future We Want: Radical Ideas for the New Century*, edited by Sarah Leonard and Bhaskar Sunkara, 1–11. New York: Metropolitan Books.

Lessig, Lawrence, and Robert McChesney. 2006. "No Tolls on the Internet." *Washington Post*, June 8. http://www.washingtonpost.com/wp-dyn/content/article/2006/06/07/AR2006060702108.html.

Levitz, Eric. 2016. "Entitled Millennial Workers of the World, Unite!" *New York*, February 4. http://nymag.com/daily/intelligencer/2016/01/entitled-millennial-workers-of-the-world-unite.html.

Long, Heather. 2013. "Forget Divestment: It's Far Better to Be an Activist Investor." *Guardian*, November 21. https://www.theguardian.com/commentisfree/2013/nov/21/fossil-fuel-company-divestment-climate-change.

Longfellow, Brenda, Glenn Richards, and Helios Design Labs. 2013. *Offshore: A Feature-Length Interactive Documentary*. 110 minutes. https://heliosdesignlabs.com/project/offshore-interactive/.

Lorin, Janet. 2015. "Who's Profiting from $1.2 Trillion of Federal Student Loans?" *Bloomberg*, December 11. https://www.bloomberg.com/news/articles/2015-12-11/a-144-000-student-default-shows-who-profits-at-taxpayer-expense.

Lukianoff, Greg, and Jonathan Haidt. 2015. "The Coddling of the American Mind." *The Atlantic*, September. https://www.theatlantic.com/magazine/archive/2015/09/the-coddling-of-the-american-mind/399356/.

Lyall, Sarah. 2016. "Trying to Pin Down the Mosaic of Millennial Tastes." *New York Times*, May 15. https://www.nytimes.com/2016/05/16/business/media/trying-to-pin-down-the-mosaic-of-millennial-tastes.html?_r=0.

Lynam, Joe. 2014. "Miliband Criticises Sports Direct Over Zero-Hours Contracts." *BBC*, November 15. http://www.bbc.com/news/uk-30069651.

Magill, Keith. 2011. "Just the Facts: Houma-Thibodaux's Economy by the Numbers." *Houma Today*, November 2. http://www.houmatoday.com/article/20111102/NEWS0101/111109857.

Mangalindan, J.P. 2015. "Snapchat's CEO on the Question He's Asked the Most: 'Why Didn't You Sell?'" *Mashable*, May 16. http://mashable.com/2015/05/16/snapchat-millennials-entitlement/#W7stDM64kOqb.

Mankiewicz, John. 2015. "Chapter 28." *House of Cards*, season 3, episode 2. Directed by John David Coles. Aired February 27.

Manne, Anne. 2014. *The Life of I: The New Culture of Narcissism*. Melbourne: Melbourne University Press.

Marcuse, Herbert. 1964. *One-Dimensional Man: Studies in the Ideology of Advanced Industrial Society*. Boston: Beacon Press.

Marcuse, Herbert. 1969. *An Essay on Liberation*. Boston: Beacon Press.

Marshall, Bob. 2014. "Losing Ground: Southeast Louisiana Is Disappearing, Quickly." *Scientific American*, August 28. https://www.scientificamerican.com/article/losing-ground-southeast-louisiana-is-disappearing-quickly/.

Martosko, David. 2015. "Trump Brings South Carolina to Its Feet with Rants on Mexico and 'Piece of Garbage' Bowe Bergdahl." *Daily Mail*, May 9. http://www.dailymail.co.uk/news/article-3075065/Trump-brings-South-Carolina-feet-rants-Mexico-State-Department-spokeswoman-s-beautiful-glasses-bab/ies-negotiate-says-don-t-sh-t-lobbyists.html.

Marx, Karl. (1867) 1976. *Capital*, vol. 1. Translated by Ben Fowkes. London: Penguin.

Marx, Karl. 1844. "Estranged Labour." *Economic and Philosophical Manuscripts of 1844*. Marxists Internet Archive, https://www.marxists.org/archive/marx/works/1844/manuscripts/labour.htm.

Maurer, Roy. 2016. "Young Job Seekers Optimistic about Gig Economy, Fear Robots at Work." Society for Human Resource Management, March 29. http://www.shrm.org/hrdisciplines/staffingmanagement/articles/pages/millennials-gig-economy-fear-robots-work.aspx.

Mazza, Ed. 2016. "Clint Eastwood Rips into 'Pussy Generation,' Says He'll Vote for Donald Trump." *Huffington Post*, August 4. http://www.huffingtonpost.com/entry/clint-eastwood-donald-trump_us_57a299c5e4b0104052a1443d.

McClennen, Sophia A. 2015. "Everyone Hates Millennials. That's Very Bad News for Student Protestors." *Washington Post*, December 15. https://www.washingtonpost.com/posteverything/wp/2015/12/15/everyone-hates-millennials-thats-very-bad-news-for-student-protesters/.

McCrate, Elaine. 2012. "Flexibility for Whom? Control over Work Schedule Variability in the US." *Feminist Economics* 18(1): 39–72. http://dx.doi.org/10.1080/13545701.2012.660179.

McDaniel. Susan, A. 2001. "Born at the Right Time? Gendered Generations and Webs of Entitlement and Responsibility." *Canadian Journal of Sociology* 26(2): 193–214. http://dx.doi.org/10.2307/3341678.

McNally, David. 2011. *Global Slump: The Economics and Politics of Crisis and Resistance*. Oakland: PM Press.

Mead, Lawrence M. 1986. *Beyond Entitlement: The Social Obligations of Citizenship*. New York: Free Press.

Meister, Jeanne. 2012. "Job Hopping is the 'New Normal' for Millennials: Three Ways to Prevent a Human Resource Nightmare." *Forbes*, August 14. https://www.forbes.com/sites/jeannemeister/2012/08/14/the-future-of-work-job-hopping-is-the-new-normal-for-millennials/#3516e472322d.

Merica, Dan. 2016. "Clinton Casts Sanders as 'Pie in the Sky' in Wisconsin." *CNN*, March 29. http://www.cnn.com/2016/03/29/politics/hillary-clinton-bernie-sanders-wisconsin/.

Messer, Olivia. 2012. "Squarely in the Red: The History behind that Felt on Your Lapel." *McGill Daily*, March 31. http://www.mcgilldaily.com/2012/03/squarely-in-the-red/.

Miller, Claire Cain. 2015. "Men Do More at Home, but Not as Much as They Think." *New York Times*, November 12. https://www.nytimes.com/2015/11/12/upshot/men-do-more-at-home-but-not-as-much-as-they-think-they-do.html?_r=1.

Mills, Charles W. 1997. *The Racial Contract*. Ithaca: Cornell University Press.

Mirrlees, Tanner. 2015. "A Critique of the Millennial: A Retreat from and Return to Class." *Alternate Routes* 26: 227–304.

Mossett, Kandi. 2015. "We Are Sacrifice Zones: Native Leader Says Dakota Fracking Fuels Violence against Women." *Democracy Now*, December 11. https://www.democracynow.org/2015/12/11/we_are_sacrifice_zones_native_leader.

Moye, David. 2015. "Millennials Are Surprisingly Chill with Funeral Selfies." *Huffington Post*, September 29. http://www.huffingtonpost.com/entry/selfie-survey-20-percent-funerals_us_5605bddee4b0af3706dc592c.

Murphy, Tim. 2015. "The Most Important Moments from Bernie Sanders' Speech Defending Democratic Socialism." *Mother Jones*, November 19. http://www.motherjones.com/politics/2015/11/bernie-sanders-socialism-speech-georgetown.

Murray, Charles. 1984. *Losing Ground: American Social Policy, 1950–1980*. New York: Basic Books.

n+1. 2015. "Meh!-lennials: On Generational Analysis." *n+1* 22(Spring). https://nplusonemag.com/issue-22/the-intellectual-situation/meh-lennials/.

NASA. 2015. "Global Temperature." *Global Climate Change: Vital Signs of the Planet*. https://climate.nasa.gov/vital-signs/global-temperature/.

National Center for Disaster Preparedness. 2016a. "SHOREline Background." http://ncdp.columbia.edu/microsite-page/shoreline/shoreline-background/.

National Center for Disaster Preparedness. 2016b. "SHOREline Home." http://ncdp.columbia.edu/microsite-page/shoreline/shoreline-home/.

National Park Service. 2016. "Jim Crow Laws." *Martin Luther King Jr. National Historic Site: Georgia.* https://www.nps.gov/malu/learn/education/jim_crow_laws.htm.

Naylor, Adrie. 2012. "Economic Crisis and Austerity: The Stranglehold on Canada's Families." *The Bullet*, April 9. http://www.socialistproject.ca/bullet/614.php.

Newstadt, Eric. 2015. "From Being an Entrepreneur to Being Entrepreneurial: The Consolidation of Neoliberalism in Ontario's Universities." *Alternate Routes* 26: 145–69.

NextGen Climate and Demos. 2016. "The Price Tag of Being Young: Climate Change and Millennials' Economic Future." http://www.demos.org/publication/price-tag-being-young-climate-change-and-millennials-economic-future.

Ng, Eddy S.W., Linda Schweitzer, and Sean T. Lyons. 2010. "New Generation, Great Expectations: A Field Study of the Millennial Generation." *Journal of Business and Psychology* 25(2): 281–92. http://dx.doi.org/10.1007/s10869-010-9159-4.

Norris, Floyd. 2014. "Corporate Profits Grow and Wages Slide." *New York Times*, April 4. https://www.nytimes.com/2014/04/05/business/economy/corporate-profits-grow-ever-larger-as-slice-of-economy-as-wages-slide.html?_r=0.

North, Anna. 2013. "Lena Dunham Isn't a Millennial." *Salon*, October 1. http://www.salon.com/2013/10/01/lena_dunham_isnt_a_millennial/.

Nozick, Robert. 1974. *Anarchy, State, and Utopia.* New York: Basic Books.

Nunberg, Geoff. 2012. "With Ryan's Ascent, a Few Thoughts on 'Entitlement.'" *NPR*, August 14. http://www.npr.org/2012/08/14/158756957/with-ryans-ascent-a-few-thoughts-on-entitlement.

Nunberg, Geoff. 2016. "Goodbye Jobs, Hello 'Gigs': How One Word Sums Up a New Economic Reality." *NPR*, January 11. http://www.npr.org/2016/01/11/460698077/goodbye-jobs-hello-gigs-nunbergs-word-of-the-year-sums-up-a-new-economic-reality.

O'Donnell, J.T. 2015. "3 Reasons Millennials Are Getting Fired." *Inc.*, August 15. http://www.inc.com/jt-odonnell/3-reasons-millennials-are-getting-fired.html.

OED. 2016a. *OED Online*, s.v. "entitlement."

OED. 2016b. *OED Online*, s.v. "entrepreneur."

OED. 2016c. *OED Online*, s.v. "myth."

O'Neill, Onara. 2008. "Nozick's Entitlements." *Inquiry* 19(1–4): 468–81.

Oxfam Canada. 2016. "There Is Enough Food to Feed the World." https://www.oxfam.ca/there-enough-food-feed-world.

Papavasileiou, Emmanouil F., and Sean T. Lyons. 2014. "A Comparative Analysis of the Work Values of Greece's 'Millennial' Generation." *International Journal of Human Resource Management* 26(17): 2166–86. http://dx.doi.org/10.1080/09585192.2014.985325.

Parramore, Lynn Stuart. 2014. "Cut-Throat Capitalism: Welcome to the Gig Economy." *AlterNet*, May 27. http://www.alternet.org/economy/cut-throat-capitalism-welcome-gig-economy.

Patel, Neil. 2015. "90% of Startups Fail: Here's What You Need to Know about the 10%." *Forbes*, January 16. https://www.forbes.com/sites/

neilpatel/2015/01/16/90-of-startups-will-fail-heres-what-you-need-to-know-about-the-10/#627771a355e1.

Pavelski, Joel. 2015. "How to Lose Your Mind and Build a Treehouse." November 8. https://medium.com/@joelcifer/how-to-build-a-treehouse-b8dd46fceb61#.oe3h5ic4n.

Pearson, Michael. 2015. "A Timeline of the University of Missouri Protests." *CNN*, November 10. http://www.cnn.com/2015/11/09/us/missouri-protest-timeline/index.html.

PEPSO (Poverty and Employment Precarity in Southern Ontario). 2013. It's More than Poverty: Employment Precarity and Household Well-Being. Summary report, February 13. https://pepsouwt.files.wordpress.com/2013/02/its-more-than-poverty-summary-feb-2013.pdf.

Pew Research Center. 2016. "Millennials." http://www.pewresearch.org/topics/millennials/.

Pickavance, Norman. 2014. "Zeroed Out: The Place of Zero-Hours Contracts in a Fair and Productive Economy." Independent report prepared for the Labour Party, United Kingdom. http://www.policyforum.labour.org.uk/uploads/editor/files/ZHCs_report_final_FINAL_240414.pdf.

Piketty, Thomas. 2014. *Capital in the Twenty-First Century*. Translated by Arthur Goldhammer. Cambridge: Cambridge University Press. http://dx.doi.org/10.4159/9780674369542.

Piven, Francis Fox. 2006. *Challenging Authority: How Ordinary People Change America*. Lanham: Rowman & Littlefield.

Pope Francis. 2015. "Encyclical letter." *Laudato Si*, no. 23, May 24. http://w2.vatican.va/content/francesco/en/encyclicals/documents/papa-francesco_20150524_enciclica-laudato-si.html.

Post, Charlie. 2015. "We're All Precarious Now." *Jacobin*, April 20. https://www.jacobinmag.com/2015/04/precarious-labor-strategies-union-precariat-standing/.

Prashad, Vijay. 2007. *The Darker Nations: A People's History of the Third World*. New York: New Press.

Prison Policy Initiative. 2016. "U.S. Incarceration Rate, 1925–2008 Prisoners per 100,000 Population." https://www.prisonpolicy.org/graphs/incarceration1925-2008.html.

Pylayev, Mariya. 2013. "Surprising Stats about Fast Food Workers." AOL.com, August 13. https://www.aol.com/article/2013/08/13/fourth-adult-fast-food-workers-are-parents/20691720/.

Quenqua, Douglas. 2013. "Seeing Narcissists Everywhere." *New York Times*, August 5. http://www.nytimes.com/2013/08/06/science/seeing-narcissists-everywhere.html?pagewanted=all&_r=0.

Raynor, Jennifer. 2016. *Generation Less: How Australia Is Cheating the Young*. Carlton: Black Inc. Books.

Robles, Frances, and Julie Bosman. 2014. "Autopsy Shows Michael Brown Was Struck at Least 6 Times." *New York Times*, August 17. https://www.nytimes.com/2014/08/18/us/michael-brown-autopsy-shows-he-was-shot-at-least-6-times.html?_r=0.

Romm, Joe. 2015. "You Just Lived through the Earth's Hottest January-April Since We Started Keeping Records." *Think Progress*, May 14. https://thinkprogress.org/climate/2015/05/14/3658741/hottest-4-month-record/.

Ross, Kristin. 2015. *Communal Luxury: The Political Imaginary of the Paris Commune*. London: Verso.

Rucker, Philip. 2011. "Romney Sees Choice Between 'Entitlement Society' and 'Opportunity Society.'" *Washington Post*, December 20. https://www.washingtonpost.com/politics/romney-sees-choice-between-entitlement-society-and-opportunity-society/2011/12/20/gIQAjXH57o_story.html?utm_term=.151c6cf9791f.

Ryan, Camille L., and Kurt Bauman. 2016. "Educational Attainment in the United States: 2015." United States Census Bureau. https://www.census.gov/content/dam/Census/library/publications/2016/demo/p20-578.pdf.

Scruton, Roger. 2012. *How to Think Seriously about the Planet: The Case for an Environmental Conservatism*. New York: Oxford University Press.

Sears, Alan. 1999. "The 'Lean' State and Capitalist Restructuring: Towards a Theoretical Account." *Studies in Political Economy* 59(1): 91–114. http://dx.doi.org/10.1080/19187033.1999.11675268.

Sears, Alan. 2003. *Retooling the Mind Factory: Education in a Lean State*. Aurora: Garamond.

Sears, Alan. 2014. *The Next New Left: A History of the Future*. Halifax: Fernwood Press.

Sears, Alan, and James Cairns. 2014. "Austerity U: Preparing Students for Precarious Lives." *New Socialist Webzine*, January 24. http://www.newsocialist.org/736-austerity-u-preparing-students-for-precarious-lives.

Sagan, Aleksandra. 2014. "Average Student Debt Difficult to Pay Off, Delays Life Milestones." *CBC News*, March 11. http://www.cbc.ca/news/canada/average-student-debt-difficult-to-pay-off-delays-life-milestones-1.2534974.

Savard, Alain, and Jerome Charaoui. 2012. "What Is an Unlimited General Student Strike?" Quebec's 2012 StudentStrike.Net. http://www.studentstrike.net/1-context/whats-an-unlimited-general-student-strike/.

Sennett, Richard. 1999. *The Corrosion of Character: The Personal Consequences of Work in the New Capitalism*. New York: WW Norton & Co.

Seymour, Richard. 2016. "Brexit: The Monkey's Paw Edition." *Lenin's Tomb*, July 5. www.leninology.co.uk/2016/07/brexit-monkeys-paw-edition.html.

Shierholz, Heidi, and Lawrence Mishel. 2013. "A Decade of Flat Wages: The Key Barrier to Shared Prosperity and a Rising Middle Class." Economic Policy Institute, August 21. http://www.epi.org/publication/a-decade-of-flat-wages-the-key-barrier-to-shared-prosperity-and-a-rising-middle-class/.

Shivani, Anis. 2016. "The Millennial Generation Is a Perfect Fit for Socialism." *AlterNet*, June 29. http://www.alternet.org/activism/millennials-perfect-fit-socialism.

Silva, Jennifer. 2013. *Coming up Short: Working-Class Adulthood in an Age of Uncertainty*. Oxford: Oxford University Press. http://dx.doi.org/10.1093/acprof:oso/9780199931460.001.0001.

Solomon, Gina M., and Sarah Janssen. 2010. "Health Effects of the Gulf Oil Spill." *Journal of the American Medical Association* 304(10): 1118–9. http://dx.doi.org/10.1001/jama.2010.1254.

Stein, Joel. 2013. "Millennials: The Me Me Me Generation." *Time*, May 20. http://time.com/247/millennials-the-me-me-me-generation/.

Strachan, Maxwell. 2014. "The U.S. Is Even More Unequal than You Realized." *Huffington Post*, May 1. http://www.huffingtonpost.com/2014/05/01/income-inequality-charts_n_5241586.html.

Stromberg, Stephen. 2016. "Bernie Sanders's Angry, Unrealistic Call for 'Revolution.'" *Washington Post*, January 18. https://www.washingtonpost.com/blogs/post-partisan/wp/2016/01/18/bernie-sanderss-angry-unrealistic-call-for-revolution/.

Stump, Kevin. 2016. "Millennials and the 2016 Election." Public lecture at Hunter College, New York, April 20.

Taylor, Kate. 2015. "Mattress Protest at Columbia University Continues into Graduation Event." *New York Times*, May 19. https://www.nytimes.com/2015/05/20/nyregion/mattress-protest-at-columbia-university-continues-into-graduation-event.html?_r=0.

Thompson, Derek. 2013. "Corporate Profits Are Eating the Economy." *The Atlantic*, March 4. https://www.theatlantic.com/business/archive/2013/03/corporate-profits-are-eating-the-economy/273687/.

Thompson, Derek. 2014. "The Incredible Shrinking Incomes of Young Americans." *The Atlantic*. December 3. https://www.theatlantic.com/business/archive/2014/12/millennials-arent-saving-money-because-theyre-not-making-money/383338/.

Thompson, Derek. 2016. "The Average 29-Year-Old." *The Atlantic*, April 20. https://www.theatlantic.com/business/archive/2016/04/the-average-29-year-old/479139/.

Times Higher Education. 2013. "Participation Rates: Now We Are 50." https://www.timeshighereducation.com/features/participation-rates-now-we-are-50/2005873.article.

Tokumitsu, Miya. 2014. "In the Name of Love." *Jacobin*, January. https://www.jacobinmag.com/2014/01/in-the-name-of-love/.

Trump, Donald. 2016. "Make America Great Again!" https://www.donaldjtrump.com/.

Tulgan, Bruce. 2009. *Not Everyone Gets a Trophy: How to Manage Generation Y*. San Francisco: Jossey-Bass.

Twenge, Jean M. 2014. *Generation Me: Why Today's Young Americans Are More Confident, Assertive, Entitled—And More Miserable than Ever Before* (rev. ed.). New York: Free Press.

Twenge, Jean M., and W. Keith Campbell. 2009. *The Narcissism Epidemic: Living in the Age of Entitlement*. New York: Free Press.

UCLA Labor Center. 2015. "Young Workers in Los Angeles." http://www.labor.ucla.edu/youngworkersla/.

Urofsky, Melvin I. 2016. "Dred Scott Decision." *Encyclopaedia Britannica*. https://www.britannica.com/event/Dred-Scott-decision.

US Department of Education. 2015. "Fast Facts: Educational Attainment." https://nces.ed.gov/fastfacts/display.asp?id=27.

US Department of Justice. 2016. "Campus Climate Survey Validation Study: Final Technical Report." *Bureau of Justice Statistics Research and Development Series*. https://www.bjs.gov/content/pub/pdf/ccsvsftr.pdf.

US Department of Labor. 2016. "National Longitudinal Surveys." Bureau of Labor Statistics. http://www.bls.gov/nls/nlsfaqs.htm#anch41.

US Government. 2015. "Inmate Race." *Federal Bureau of Prisons*, August 29. https://www.bop.gov/about/statistics/statistics_inmate_race.jsp.

van Gelder, Sarah, ed. 2011. *This Changes Everything: Occupy Wall Street and the 99% Movement*. San Francisco: Barrett-Koehler Publishers.

Vogel, Lise. (1983) 2014. *Marxism and the Oppression of Women: Toward a Unitary Theory*. Chicago: Haymarket Books.

Walsh, Katie. 2015. "'Fort Tilden' Rips into Millennial Culture with a Beach Day from Hell." *Los Angeles Times*, August 13. http://www.latimes.com/entertainment/movies/la-et-mn-fort-tilden-movie-review-20150814-story.html.

Walsh, Kenneth T. 2016. "Young People Favor Bernie Sanders, Socialism." *U.S. News*, February 19. https://www.usnews.com/news/blogs/ken-walshs-washington/2016/02/19/young-people-favor-bernie-sanders-socialism.

Wanjuki, Wagatwe. 2014. "RAINN'S Recommendations Ignore Needs of Campus Survivors of All Identities." *Feministing*. http://feministing.com/2014/03/14/response-to-rainn-campus-rape-recommendations/.

We Are the 99 Percent. 2011a. http://wearethe99percent.tumblr.com/post/11705237894/sorry-for-the-poor-quality-its-all-i-have-im.

We Are the 99 Percent. 2011b. http://wearethe99percent.tumblr.com/post/11694421937/i-am-24-i-have-over-100k-in-student-loan-debt.

We Are the 99 Percent. 2011c. http://wearethe99percent.tumblr.com/post/11651923675/i-have-a-master-of-arts-degree-in-womens-studies.

Weeks, Kathi. 2011. *The Problem with Work: Feminism, Marxism, Anti-Work Politics, and Postwork Imaginaries*. Durham: Duke University Press. http://dx.doi.org/10.1215/9780822394723.

Wente, Margaret. 2013. "Student Debt Crisis? No, Expectations Crisis." *Globe and Mail*, October 31. http://www.theglobeandmail.com/opinion/student-debt-crisis-twas-ever-thus/article15166915/.

West, Lindy. 2015. "Trigger Warnings Don't Hinder Freedom of Expression: They Expand It." *Guardian*, August 18. https://www.theguardian.com/education/commentisfree/2015/aug/18/trigger-warnings-dont-hinder-freedom-expression.

Widdicombe, Ben. 2016. "What Happens When Millennials Run the Workplace?" *New York Times*, March 19. https://www.nytimes.com/2016/03/20/fashion/millennials-mic-workplace.html?_r=1&module=ArrowsNav&contentCollection=Fashion%20%26%20Style&action=keypress&region=FixedLeft&pgtype=article.

Wieczner, Jen. 2014. "10 Things Generation Y Won't Tell You." *MarketWatch*, August 21. http://www.marketwatch.com/story/10-things-millennials-wont-tell-you-2013-06-21.

Williams, Chris. 2010. *Ecology and Socialism: Solutions to Capitalism Ecological Crisis*. Chicago: Haymarket.

Williams, Ray. 2014. "How the Millennial Generation Will Change the World of Work." *Financial Post*, March 19. http://business.financialpost.com/executive/careers/how-the-millennial-generation-will-change-the-world-of-work.

Wilson, Jennifer. 2015. "How Black Lives Matter Saved Higher Education." *Al Jazeera America*, December 31. http://america.aljazeera.com/opinions/2015/12/how-black-lives-matter-saved-higher-education.html.

Wilson, Shaun, and Norbert Ebert. 2013. "Precarious Work: Economic, Sociological and Political Perspectives." *Economic and Labour Relations Review* 24(3): 263–78. http://dx.doi.org/10.1177/1035304613500434.

Wolff, Richard. 2012. *Democracy at Work: A Cure for Capitalism*. Chicago: Haymarket Books.

Wong, Alia. 2015. "The Renaissance of Student Activism." *The Atlantic*, May 21. https://www.theatlantic.com/education/archive/2015/05/the-renaissance-of-student-activism/393749.

Woodard, Komozi. 2011. "'Want to Start a Revolution?' Radical Women in the Black Freedom Struggle." Public Lecture at Ryerson University, Toronto, Ontario, March 1.

Workers Action Centre. 2016. "Minimum Wage." http://www.workersactioncentre.org/issues/minimum-wage/.

Wright, Kai. 2015. "Black Lives Matter Is a Demand, Not a Plea." *The Nation*, August 12. https://www.thenation.com/article/black-lives-matter-is-a-demand-not-a-ple.

Younglai, Rachelle. 2016. "For Young Canadians, a New Reality: Dealing with 'Job Churn.'" *Globe and Mail*, October 28. http://www.theglobeandmail.com/report-on-business/economy/jobs/canadian-youth-working-low-paid-temporary-jobs/article32579528/.

Zaslow, Jeffrey. 2007a. "Blame It on Mr. Rogers: Why Young Adults Feel So Entitled." *Wall Street Journal*, July 5. https://www.wsj.com/articles/SB118358476840657463.

Zaslow, Jeffrey. 2007b. "The Entitlement Epidemic: Who's Really to Blame?" *Wall Street Journal*, July 19. https://www.wsj.com/articles/SB118480432643571003.

Zinshteyn, Mikhail. 2016. "College Freshmen Are More Politically Engaged than They Have Been in Decades." *FiveThirtyEight*, February 11. https://fivethirtyeight.com/features/college-freshmen-are-more-politically-engaged-than-they-have-been-in-decades/.

Zweig, Michael. 2006. "Six Points on Class." *Monthly Review* 58(3): 116. https://monthlyreview.org/2006/07/01/six-points-on-class/.

INDEX